'Execution on Duty'

Murder or misadventure in Plymouth

by
Peter D Hume

This book is dedicated to the memory

of

Police Constable 45 William Bennett

Plymouth Borough Police

A sudden change, he unexpected fell
He had no time to bid his wife or friends farewell
Think nothing strange death awaits us all
His lot today, tomorrow thine may fall.

{Inscription on PC Bennett's' Gravestone}

Contents

Foreword	5
Chapter 1.	6
Chapter 2	21
Chapter 3	42
Chapter 4	50
Chapter 5	68
Chapter 6	78
Chapter 7	92
Chapter 8	98
Chapter 9	106
Chapter 10	116
Chapter 11	130
Chapter 12	141
Chapter 13	152
Chapter 14	161
Chapter 15	174
Chapter 16	189
Chapter 17	201
Chapter 18	205

Chapter 20	249
Chapter 21	256
Chapter 22	266
Chapter 23	301
Chapter 24	314
Chapter 25	318
Chapter 26	323

This book is based on real events and people. Where possible the events have been researched and detailed as accurately as possible. This book is a fictional novel by definition as the dialogues and characterisations are the result of the author's interpretation and imagination.

Foreword

The time is the present. I'm standing in Ford Park Cemetery Plymouth.

Originally the Plymouth, Devonport and Stonehouse Cemetery it opened in 1848 and at that time was on the outskirts of the local towns boundaries.

I'm staring at an ornate well weathered headstone, marking the grave of Constable William Bennett a twenty-five-year-old Plymouth Borough Policeman.

I read the carefully chiselled inscription and this set my mind racing, I needed to know more. What was behind his untimely death?

This opening might seem a little strange to those that don't know me.

I was born in Plymouth and served as a detective in the City and have long held a passion for the city's history, and my own family history which had initially led me to this location.

This was the start of my quest to record Constable Bennetts fateful story.

Chapter 1.

July 1875; the sun was high in Plymouth and for a few weeks had been heating up the cobbled streets. Rain was badly needed to wash them down, but there was no immediate sign of any change to the weather.

The town, Devon's main port boasted a long maritime and military history, and together with the two adjoining towns of Stonehouse and Devonport, made up the area known locally as the 'Three Towns'

High Street ran from Whimple Street, across Notte Street, ending at the Parade on the Barbican. It was a busy commercial area housing a large number of local businesses, with mixed dwellings running off and backing on to the area.

Numerous shops and beer houses were scattered along both sides of the street. These catered for the needs of the traders, visitors, poor locals and some who ventured to the area, normally in search of pleasures of the flesh.

Daily life in the street could be described as full of noise, smells, and characters.

Michael Oleman, known as 'Fishy Mick' was the name most locals knew him as. His only clothes carried the scent of his casual work. This led to him not being welcome in some of the surrounding business premises.

Mick stood on the corner of High Street and Lower Lane. He chewed for a while then spat out the piece of nail bitten off his already damaged thumb nail and leant against the wall pretending to look bored but was carefully watching the street for opportunity.

Mick spent a lot of time watching and listening around the High-Street area. In fact, this had become more of a daily routine than ever his quest for work as a fishing boat deck hand, and if his luck was in, sometimes more profitable.

He sniffed the air; the heat had increased the levels of street smells that came from the poorly kept drains and channels used to carry the waste and water. The closeness to the Barbican area, home of the local fishing fleet, added to the odour. He was used to this but to non-locals the smell of fish could remain in your nostrils for days, today it hung in the air.

The reason this area had become Mick's favourite was that he needed to make money, and this was a busy street, just right at times for his thieving. He liked to drink; this required money, and he didn't mind how he came by it. His old skills learnt in the past had not been forgotten.

Like many others, Mick had originally moved to Liverpool with his father, nearly 30 years before, following the potato famine in his Irish homeland. They had travelled on one of the perilously overloaded crafts across the Irish Sea. They survived unlike some of their fellow countrymen travelling on the so called wooden coffin ships to America.

Their arrival in Liverpool found them having to live in the crowded stagnant water filled cellars near the docks, along with the many other immigrants. The arrival of so many people had increased the problems in the town. Disease was rife amongst the cellar inhabitants and it was not long before his father became one of the many cholera victims. His father's death was a shock to Mick, but he soon learnt ways of his own to steal, survive, and avoid the authorities. Thieving was his only option or joining the inevitable death toll that increased daily. He managed to avoid being sent back to Ireland by dodging the authorities when new laws on deportation were passed, by keeping out of the way and, although his life was grim, he was a survivor. The dockland area of Liverpool eventually started to expand and recover, enabling Mick to make the right move and obtain regular work as a deck hand in the docks various ships. He had arrived in Plymouth several months ago, on a cargo boat that had called in for an emergency repair to its rudder, on its way from Liverpool to Africa. His life though had suddenly changed direction again after becoming drunk one night in High

Street's ale houses and missing his boat sailing and losing all his worldly goods - or so he assumed. He later found out they had been left by the skipper on the quayside prior to sailing, but there was little chance now of ever knowing where they had gone, somebody had come across a lucky find.

Mick's arrival in Plymouth, other than through his own circumstances, was not unusual. The population had increased with an influx of Irish, along with people from poorly paid farming areas and the declining Cornish mines.

They all originally had dreams of finding work but, like all dreams, reality was sometimes a different matter.

Mick's casual work when it happened, and he had the inclination, was a bonus. As well as watching and listening in the street he couldn't help but notice the people just like himself, that were wandering aimlessly about without work, all of them looking for other ways to make money to survive. The difference between the poor, struggling to survive, and the well-off was very clear to see, and he was more than aware he was now one of them.

Mick having lived in the poorest part of Liverpool for some time had no fears about venturing into the lanes leading off the High Street; he found that the life here was no different - it also painted a grim picture though. Delving into these lanes and alleyways as he wandered revealed many stories of violence, hardship and alcoholism, amongst its mixed inhabitants. The lanes also had their fair share of wildlife, being the haunts of numerous stray dogs and wild cats - though it was questionable where they sometimes disappeared. Some suggested that they were occasionally a ready ingredient for the cook pot. These animals in turn managed to survive on the never-ending supply of fresh meat from the rats.

Mick's first task, when he found he had missed his boat, was to search for his belongings and after he had fully recovered from his drunken stupor, his intention was to try and find a room to stay - though he had little money. He wandered off the high Street finding himself amongst the poorly constructed houses that were black faced from the smoke of household fires and were badly in need of repairs to windows and roofs. He knocked on doors but the squalid houses, with shared sanitation, were already cramped with families forced to share small rooms with numerous other families occupying one house. Privacy was scarce, with very little in the way of secrets being kept, news travelled fast in the area of Plymouth's High Street. Mick slept rough for most of the time around the Barbican - finding shelter in some boats that were being stored on the quay, which suited him as he was close to and able to keep an eye on the fishing boats for work, when not celebrating his latest illegal gain of money of course. During his wanderings, he met some fellow countrymen who were working locally on the railway; they had of course welcomed and accepted him, and with their help, he got employment 'track laying'. This had only lasted a few months as now, having a steady wage, his increased drinking and regular lateness for work led to him being laid off and thus losing his bed in the shared room, and once more it was back to the boats again for sleeping.

Mick looked up and down the High Street but watched closely an old man begging. He thought to himself the old man may help him as well and be an easy way of getting some money without any violence, as the man didn't look too difficult to overcome. Mick needed money and would steal, but violence was not his game - just perhaps a gentle push or shove and a hand in the pocket would meet his needs.

The old man leant against the wall, scratching his whiskered dirty face trying to catch his breath. 'Coins' he mumbled; but he thought people were ignoring him, or perhaps there was nobody there, he couldn't really tell. He squinted through reddened eyes and thrust a grubby hand towards any movement he thought came towards him, not now bothering to speak, just fixing his face with a threatening stare. He despised this street. He'd had enough of it, and hated anyone who didn't give to him, and he badly needed a drink. He was shaking and he knew drink was the only way to stop the tremors taking over his body, and perhaps ease his pains. His life had been the sea and this clearly showed in his ruddy salt burned face. He was though past all that now, having drunk too much for longer than he cared to remember. Crippled from an accident at sea and continually wracked with pain from his badly treated foot injury, he coughed and spat blood on the road as he shuffled away from the wall - slowly dragging along his blistered and sore right foot. Supporting himself against the wall he walked with difficulty, trying also to ignore the chest pain, and cursing loudly about the street and everyone who walked it. His brain was addled with drink but every so often he thought he recognised parts of the street - but then these thoughts quickly faded, he must be imagining it. If he was capable of thinking straight he couldn't even remember how he got there, or more importantly why he was there.

A group of fishermen who were used to the local smells, and had just returned from sea, noisily made their way from the Barbican making for the taverns to celebrate their catch and earnings. Mick saw them and stood back in a doorway trying to hide his face, just in case he knew some of them. The old man had heard them and thrust out his hand, but they had crossed the street away from him. He mumbled a curse, not knowing where they had gone. They though were eager to reach some of the ale houses in High Street to quench their thirsts and rid their throats of the salty sea taste that had accumulated from days on the sea.

As well as playing in the streets it was common to also see children wandering around the adjoining lanes off High Street looking for ways to earn or steal. Anything would sell - it didn't have to be money they searched for.

The old man forced his way past two young boys who were thin, hungry and shoeless, wearing dirty ragged patched clothes. They were carrying pieces of wood, using them as swords, playing near a lane. Their pretend game of pirates, mixed with their shouts and the clatter of their make-believe swords, irritated him and, as he approached them, he wasn't sure what they were doing. Startled by the noise, he shouted at them - cursing and waving his arms for them to move out of his way - as he stumbled past them into the lane. The boys ran off looking for new mischief and make-believe adventures to occupy them, stopping and shouting back at him when they were a safe distance away. These boys were fortunate, as the mortality rate amongst children was high. Families had as many as ten children, sometimes more, and some children would not survive, as a simple cold could often lead to death.

The old man heard them running and shouting as he limped into the lane, supporting himself with his right arm against the wall.

His mind was confused, and the pain was increasing in his arm and chest. He clutched his chest as he fell heavily amongst the rubbish.

Mick had seen him enter the lane and decided to move slowly in that direction and, as he approached the lane, he saw someone else who he knew by sight from the ale houses quickly follow the old man into the lane. He stopped and waited on the opposite side of the street thinking that perhaps he had been beaten at his own game.

The person who had followed the old man was also desperate for money, they had heard him cry out as he fell, but had no intention of helping him and they had also been watching him for some time. He would be found later, hopefully before the heat increased, or the rats discovered him.

A quick pair of hands ran over the old man's clothing feeling for movement but, more importantly, for any valuables he may have. There was no sign of any breathing. He was dead, and they were fast in their search feeling his pockets whilst, at the same time, glancing furtively around for any signs of others. Their luck was in as a locket, secured around his neck with dirty cord, was found and roughly removed. There was no guilt in their actions; he wouldn't need it now they thought. Clutching the locket tightly they hurried away to an adjoining alleyway where they stopped to examine their find. A smile came over their face on seeing that the round locket appeared to be silver coloured, although tarnished and dirty. It would hopefully make some money later. Thrusting it inside their clothing for safe keeping, they moved quickly from the lane in the opposite direction, looking over their shoulder and around them, checking continually to see that nobody had seen them. They made their way into the High Street and moved quickly amongst the crowds, where nobody would take any notice, and then walked away. Unknown to them Mick had seen them and he thought 'if all else fails' an approach to them may also be a possible easy way of receiving a coin or two for his trouble.

Once in their room the thief moved a bed away from the wall, prized up the small, loose, section of the floor with their dirty nails - all the time listening out for movement outside the door whilst they hid the locket and replaced the bed. This hiding place had been used many times previously; the locket would remain there until they knew that nobody would be looking for it, or them. It was too soon to try and sell the locket, even though the money was needed. They sat on the bed and sucked the blood away from a small cut on the end of their finger, caused by lifting the flooring, and they could smile again thinking about the locket. Perhaps today their luck was in at last, but not just yet they would have to wait.

Mick made his way into the lane, immediately seeing the old man lying on the ground but fear gripped him as he looked towards the body of the man lying there; he turned, quickly making his way out of the lane. If the old man was dead, and he certainly looked like he could be, there was no way he wanted to be involved, but he knew of someone who perhaps was, and thought again that he may make an approach once he saw them.

He returned to the High Street, waiting and watching to see what might happen, still fearful that he himself may have been seen. He needed to find out, as it may be necessary for him to leave Plymouth. He did not have to wait long in his watch on the lane, he saw a boy run from the lane towards the top of High Street shouting 'Police come quick' and realised the old man's body had been found. Mick waited around keeping himself in a doorway but knew he could find out soon what was known.

Chapter 2

Plymouth and particularly the High-street area had its share of petty crime. There were a number of people who liked to think of the street as their very own territory, but they very much disliked the closeness of the Police House.

The Police House, containing cells for prisoners, usually appearing in court the next day, was at the top of High Street. It was well known to some but those whose history of crime was lengthy feared the Borough Prison more. This was situated near the workhouse in the Greenbank area of town. This had a reputation for harshness and was somewhere to be avoided as far as they were concerned.

Fishy Mick generally liked to work on his own, but he was aware of and knew most of a small group of locals who considered it part of their daily routine to pit their wits against the risk of arrest and being locked in the cells. Necessity, in order to survive, was their excuse to steal. It had almost become a challenge to them;

the Police were fair game and to be able to outwit them without being arrested was something they delighted in bragging about in the ale houses, spending the coins they had managed to acquire. There were also those who liked to smile and listen to the conversations going on around them. Perhaps this easily found knowledge could be used to their advantage, and money could be made in other ways.

PC45 William Bennett, of the Plymouth Borough Police, who had transferred from the Devonport Borough Police, had quickly got to know the High-Street area and its locals well. Following the move from Devonport a lot had happened. Jane, the servant girl he had met at Devonport and fallen in love with, had moved with the family she worked for to their new house, but her work was still close by, which would work out well for her and William. Their relationship had grown, which was no surprise to those that knew them. This was followed a few months later by his Marriage to her. They had been married a few months and had recently moved into a house in Hampton Street, which was within walking distance of Will's work. On her marriage, Jane had to give up work, but they were happy that they were able to survive on his Police pay along with some money given at the time of their marriage; their future looked good, with plans for a family.

He had been patrolling the same area since his arrival the previous year, it had become his patch and he made sure that he in turn was known in the area. To his surprise, he found that he had quickly developed a certain amount of fondness for the area. It was busier than his previous Devonport beats and he had built up a degree of respect amongst some of the locals. This had arisen through dealing with some of the problems in their premises and he had learnt to his satisfaction that he was considered a firm but fair officer. Yes, here was somebody they could trust and this was something he was quite proud of. Bennett would spend time talking to the locals, gathering snippets of information as to what was happening and what they had heard. All this was logged in his memory and used to assist himself and his colleagues in carrying out their work.

Of course, there was a group who definitely did not share the same views, who watched from various doorways, and other vantage points, hoping they hadn't been seen as he walked at his regulation pace -having left the Police Station and entered the top of High Street.

He was working from 5.00 p.m. until 9.00 p.m. and was looking forward to spending some time later with his wife.

PC Bennett paused at the top of the street, taking in the smell of the warm air mixed with the familiar cocktail of obnoxious smells. He flexed his toes in his new boots, worn for the first time today, hoping it would stretch the leather, and ease the pain in some of his toes. He prided himself on his smart upright appearance and walked, with his hands linked behind his back, down the slight slope of the road - deliberately walking in the centre – and thinking to himself "I know exactly what they will be doing." He had of course seen them all and knew his presence would arouse their interest, choosing to ignore their glances. Let them play their little games. He walked past the Napoleon Inn on his right, pausing slightly and glancing towards it out of habit, and did the same as he passed the Naval Reserve Inn further down on his left. Whilst working, he had been to these ale houses on numerous occasions. Both premises were reasonably quiet at this time of day, but PC Bennett knew that later in his shift there would be a lot more activity in and around them probably keeping him busy. His watchers particularly Mick carefully continued to look where he was going and a few followed at a safe distance, using other doorways to loiter in, but they were eager to find out what he was up to. Mick of course had a vested interest and was more eager than most but he didn't want to show it.

PC 45 had been sent to a lane off High Street, following a

frightened pale faced errand boy running into the Police Station, blurting out between gasps of breath and sobs that he had found the body of a man amongst rubbish at the rear of a shop. Bennett had only entered a short distance into the lane before he saw the man lying on his left side amongst the rubbish. Kneeling down he felt for a pulse in the neck, immediately being hit by the stale sweaty smell of the man and the strong smell of drink mixed with urine. To try and breathe some fresher air he turned his head away for a while. Carefully examining the body for breathing, obvious signs of injury, and then searching the clothing for belongings, he found no injuries and a complete lack of any belongings. Standing up PC Bennett looked down at the man; he was obviously dead, but still slightly warm to the touch. He felt a pang of sorrow for him, thinking how his life had ended lying in a pile of rubbish, and wondered if anybody would care - or would this man be another 'unknown' placed in a pauper's grave. By the time, PC Bennett had finished his examination a few of the locals, along with some of the shopkeepers, had gathered at the entrance to the lane eager to see what was happening, but not wanting and careful not to get involved. He turned and walked towards them, causing several to instinctively move to the back of the crowd in the hope they wouldn't be noticed. "Does anybody know who this man is" asked PC Bennett in his clear authoritative voice?

Mick had joined the crowd at the back listening more than watching to find out what was known, he kept his head looking down, trying not to show his face.

Nobody replied or wanted to say anything in case it meant becoming involved. He then said in a louder voice "Somebody must have seen him in the area?" Somebody had in fact been very close to him, very carefully watching events from the back of the crowd and, after seeing and hearing what was happening, moved silently away. It would appear neither he nor the other person had been seen. He made his way to the Barbican feeling happier at what he had seen and heard, perhaps someone would buy him a drink, and he would definitely keep out of High Street for a few days.

Charlie Simpson - the local fishmonger who was stood at the front of the crowd - looked up and said, "Yes, he's been in the street begging and being a general nuisance. I first saw him yesterday, but don't know nothing about him and I've been working around this area long enough to get to know everyone who is a local."

Several of the crowd then joined in the conversation, nodding and agreeing with what was said, but nobody wanted to or was able to identify this old man. Helping the Police was not what most of them would do, and losing interest, they drifted away to take their chances in search of more productive activities.

Pc Bennett was joined by a colleague, who he left at the entrance to the lane whilst he himself made enquiries in the area with the other shopkeepers, and at some of the nearby addresses. Nobody seemed to know anything, but several had also seen the man begging in the area in the last few days. Further enquiries would have to be made to try and identify him and any possible family. PC Bennett having completed his enquiries decided it was time to return to the station, arrange for the police surgeon, and for the removal of the body by stretcher to the mortuary for a post mortem. The local newspapers would carry a description for him, and he carefully filled out the form describing the incident for the coroner, briefing his sergeant on what had taken place.

William Bennett, or Will as he liked to be known, was brought up in the area of Landrake Cornwall, a few miles from Plymouth. It was a rural area, consisting of a scattering of cottages with most of the locals being employed in agriculture.

He grew up within a family who were involved in the local community and, as with most villages they knew everyone. All the locals certainly knew Will. He attended the village school, generally enjoying it and being described as 'an above average pupil' with a strong sense of right and wrong. He helped out on the farms after school and during holidays when he could, but Will's boyhood ambition had always been to join the Police. He wanted to get away from what he considered to be a routine that had no future, not wanting to end up working on a farm, as most that left school did. Everyone thought he would make an ideal policeman, he had the build and the ability to talk easily to whoever he met; he could never be described as quiet. He used to talk about nothing else, and he would talk to the local policeman whenever he saw him. Despite his outgoing personality, Will was in awe of him initially. He would stare at the police uniform and just be amazed at how tall the PC looked with his helmet on. He gradually built up enough courage to speak, asking him questions about what he did, and how he could become a policeman when he was older. It became a regular thing for Will to look out for the policeman and he always wanted to know if he had any adventures to tell him about. These questions caused great amusement but were answered with some slight embellishment to make his 'routine rural beat' sound more exciting to a young boy. Will wanted to better himself and seek some adventure; he couldn't wait to leave school.

Even though he was from a country background he felt that working in a town area would provide more challenges and adventure for him and the possible opportunity for advancement, this was his dream.

He could clearly remember making his way for his interview with the Superintendent, crossing the River Tamar by ferry boat, and then the long walk to the Devonport Borough Police Station. His meeting had gone well. Backed by good references and a school report, he had been accepted subject to his medical with the force surgeon. He was more nervous before this than at the interview but need not have worried as his build and height was what they were looking for and, following a thorough examination, Will Bennett was declared medically fit. He described his acceptance as the proudest day of his life, and he couldn't wait to get back to his village to let his family know.

The big day came, and Will joined the Devonport Borough Police.

He felt even prouder the day he was issued with his uniform and equipment, smiling as he tried it on with the pill box type hat; at last "I look like a policeman" he thought. He realised though there were lots more to do and learn before he could proudly start work on the streets.

His initial acceptance had been followed by training in the law and learning the procedures. Will found all this hard to start with, particularly living away from home for the first time, but his perseverance and long hours spent studying led to the eventual day he was allowed out onto the streets of Devonport.

To start with he was accompanied by experienced officers who showed him the beats with their own peculiarities and problems. Will learnt very quickly from them the art of policing the various areas, including - most importantly - where refreshment could also be obtained.

Because of his build, he was able to look after himself. This was borne out particularly working in the region of the Dockyard, where regular trouble occurred in the ale houses. It was accepted locally that the Police in the area were more than capable of sorting out drunks and trouble makers.

Will's willingness to get involved endeared him to his colleagues, made him a popular member of the force, and he was readily accepted into his section.

In addition to the regular assaults, drunkenness, and domestic issues that occurred, a lot of time was taken up dealing with families and children who were not attending school. This was a major problem within the area.

Lodgings had been found for him with a family in keyham,

where he occupied a room but, when off duty ate with the family.

Most of his little off duty time he sat in his room brushing up on the law, priding himself on his new found knowledge and keen to put it into practice.

There were some aspects of policing that weren't easy and dealing with death was something that couldn't be taught. Will soon learnt from his colleagues that they all had differing ways of handling the many issues that could arise. He found that nobody he worked with had disrespect for the dead, always realising that a member of someone's family was involved but humour would sometimes creep in, either at the time or in discussions afterwards. This was a way to relieve any stress brought about by the sometimes-horrific incidents they had to deal with. Early in his career Will had two experiences that stuck with him.

His first experience involved a visit by the local undertaker and his assistant who called at the Police Station seeking help to remove a body from a house. The man had been examined by his doctor and death had been certified, but they needed assistance to move the body from a difficult area. This was an unusual request, but he was detailed to assist by a Sergeant quietly smiling to himself and thinking, 'this will be a good initiation for the boy'. With a certain amount of trepidation, Will arrived at a house to find that the body was that of a man at least 19 or 20 stone in weight. He was lying on a bed in an upstairs room, reached only by a small narrow winding staircase, with a sharp turn in the middle. The undertaker decided that the man would be placed on their canvas sheet, with attached handles, 'somehow' to be taken down the stairs. The three men managed to get the man onto the sheet. Then came the difficult part. After several unsuccessful attempts, due to the narrow stairs and the annoying turn in them half way down, they decided that the assistant would take the feet end of the sheet, and the undertaker and Will would hold the handles at the top behind the head. Fortunately for them there was no family present and, as they were unable to fully lift the body off the ground because of the weight and the lack of space, they managed to bump it down the stairs to the hall below. The curve in the stairs was achieved by bending the body and forcing it around the narrow bend. When they reached the hall, they were hot and sweating and so relieved to be able to finally put the body on the floor. Will soon learnt that air can be contained in a body for a certain time. As the body came to rest on the floor the bumping had caused the air inside to be expelled through the dead man's mouth and there was a sudden aaaaaaagh causing Will to jump with shock. The other two just laughed it off. Will tried to recover quickly when he realised what had happened and did his best to hide his reddened face. This was the first incident with a dead body and he certainly didn't want to brag about it to any of his colleagues.

The second incident came shortly afterwards, when Will was directed to attend the local mortuary to remove a ring from an elderly lady's body. The lady had died in the street, and her family lived nearby. They had called at the station to collect her belongings, taken from her at the mortuary. They examined them but were concerned about a valuable ring which she wore. The ring though was not amongst her belongings and its return was requested. The desk officer knew that there was no problem regarding the ring as he had been informed it was still on the lady's finger, being too difficult to remove. With his wicked sense of humour again, the desk officer knew just the person for the job.

The key for the mortuary was kept at the Police station, and Will duly collected it from the station sergeant. He had attended the mortuary previously but had always been accompanied and didn't relish going there alone. Fortunately, it was still daylight. Will unlocked the mortuary, leaving the door open, feeling a little bit easier by doing this. He knew that the body had been there awaiting a post mortem, and the room was cold and smelt stale. There was not a lot of room inside. As he entered he saw the body on the marble slab, covered in a sheet, with the head facing towards him. The ring, he had been told, was on the right hand, which would make his job easier, as he wouldn't have to walk around the body. He stood beside the body pulled the sheet down exposing the top half of the body and slowly lifted the arm, relieved to find the ring was still there. Catching hold of the cold hand he wriggled the ring but it only moved slightly and, no matter how hard he tried, it would not shift from the finger. He thought to himself, no wonder they didn't take it off with the rest of her belongings. The ring was old and thin and had moulded itself with wear to the shape of the lady's finger. Will looked around, eager to resolve the problem and get outside again. Thinking he would dampen the finger with water to make it slippery, he placed the arm back on the edge of the slab.

Turning to his right he saw there was a metal jug of water on the floor. As he bent over suddenly he felt a thump on his lower back. Will didn't look to see what had happened, but just jumped and ran straight out of the mortuary door. He got outside into the courtyard and slowly looked over his shoulder, to his relief seeing there was nothing behind him. Panting he stopped and looked back towards the door, trying to think what had frightened him, and of course thinking 'pull yourself together.' He looked out towards the street, hoping that nobody had seen him run out, and felt relief that there wasn't anyone to be seen. Will walked slowly back towards the door, stopped and gingerly looked inside not knowing what to expect and feeling relieved when he saw that the arm had fallen off the edge of the slab, swung down, and this is what had hit him in the back. How stupid he felt at being scared so easily and carried on with his original plan - finding the water eventually did the trick - and he easily slid the ring off the lady's hand.

Will locked the mortuary door, feeling more at ease having completed the task. He decided he definitely wouldn't tell anybody about his 'little' experience, he was just too embarrassed and annoyed with himself.

PC Bennett enjoyed his time working around Devonport but in November 1873 he had applied, and successfully transferred, to the Plymouth Borough Police. This move had come about as he had been wanting to work in Plymouth; he had met and talked to others who worked there and felt it would be a different way of life. It was a busier area with more commercial premises and people. The move became even more essential after his meeting with a young servant girl named Mary Jane Hooper, but known as Jane. She worked in one of the large houses in his area and they had met when he had called at the house dealing with a theft of food from the outside larder. There seemed to be an instant attraction and Will made numerous calls to the house when he was working that locality, telling them he was keeping an eye open in the area He knew his visits though were to see Jane, or at least he hoped to see her if she wasn't too busy. There was always a drink and some cake for him in the kitchen, and the cook used to smile as she knew what he was really calling for. He soon learnt when Jane had her time off and tended to time his visits to coincide with her free time.

They could then meet for a short time in between her duties. Days off were rare for Jane and her working hours were long, but they did meet whenever possible. Will was upset when one afternoon she told him she was moving into Plymouth with the family as they were buying a larger house.

He wasted no time in requesting a transfer and was delighted when it was approved. He couldn't wait to tell Jane. It couldn't be better and was pleased when he found he would be working from the station house in the Guildhall it would be busier, and he would be again near to Jane.

Chapter 3

Susan Foster, a convicted thief and prostitute, knew Plymouth High Street and the adjoining lanes well. She could certainly be included amongst the regulars who frequented the area. Most days she could be found either trying to steal or plying her trade as a prostitute amongst her regular punters or visitors to the area. She occupied a scruffy, poorly kept, downstairs room - her only room - at 5 Lower Lane which ran off the High Street. She was a local woman having spent most of her life working and living in various houses that adjoined the main street. Susan at 22 was very street wise and knew most of the locals and various undesirables who frequented the area. She was generally drunk, not liked, loud, but tolerated at times when the drink didn't rule her brain. She did though still have a few people in the area that she could rely on, more through pity than anything.

She was well known to the Police, having had numerous court appearances, and Susan was once described in a local paper following a court case as *'a woman of ill fame, well known to the Police for her thieving and fighting propensities. She has a very repulsive appearance and is rarely without a bandaged head or black eye"*

Susan had once been an attractive dark-haired woman, but her lifestyle and constant fight to survive had made her look older. She was thin, her skin being pale and dirty looking. Her eyes possessed a haunted look, continually darting in different directions, borne from her instinct to survive and avoid arrest. Her health had suffered, she knew that she drank too much, and never bothered to take care of herself. There were times, when she was sober, that she wished she could escape her life, but the following day the cycle of drinking and willing men would start again.

Lack of washing facilities meant body odour was normal amongst the locals, but she tried to wash every week and had found that, particularly during the warm weather, she was able to bathe naked in a small cove close to the Barbican. She had discovered this hideaway as a young girl; it was something she had not shared with anyone, nor wanted to. She did not though relish the rats and wild cats that frequented the area, having at times to navigate through them whilst climbing up and down to the small rocky beach area. Susan enjoyed this freedom; it was somewhere where she could lose herself and think about her life or lack of it - particularly when she was sober. She spent as long as she dared away from prying eyes and the hustle of the street and her grim existence. She was normally able to enjoy her bathing without anyone disturbing her, only occasionally being shouted and whistled at from passing boats. This did not bother her as her body had been seen and abused by more men than she cared to remember.

Susan couldn't remember her father; she told her that when she was born her Father doted on her but he had been lost at sea when she was young. She wasn't sure if this was right as her mother never had too much to say about him, even when she was asked. She did know that, at one time, they lived a reasonable life and could remember happier times when she was younger. She would smile thinking about how her mother always called her 'Foss'. This apparently had been one of the first words that she had said and for some reason the name had stuck and was always used by her Father, but few now seemed to use it. Following the disappearance of her Father, her mother started to drink and their lifestyle went downhill rapidly. Money became scarcer, the drinking increased, and her Mother eventually died. Susan and her sister Nancy were heartbroken and it resulted in a pauper's funeral; the girls had no money to pay for the unmarked grave.

They were left having no known relatives to support them, and in the early days there were some eager to take advantage of vulnerable young girls, wanting to use them for work or their own pleasure.

The girls were eventually evicted from the two rooms in Looe Street they had occupied with their Mother. It was only through the help of their mother's long-time friend Maisie that they were initially given free lodgings. By doing this they had managed to avoid the authorities and the possibility of the local orphanage. They were able to stay there whilst they found somewhere to live, but this of course would require them to earn money in some way.

Employment was scarce, particularly for women; the girls sought any work - which they then supplemented by begging and stealing food. Life was hard, and the inevitable happened. In order to survive, both girls drifted into working the streets as prostitutes. Susan knew the majority of prostitutes in the area and most had started working when they were about 15. Some she knew were younger, and others took further risks and ignored the legal age of 12. Those that had minders found this to be a way of forcing them to earn extra money. There were plenty of men willing to pay good money for young girls.

This existence gave Susan and her sister a living of sorts, and they were always careful to look out for each other.

The dangers of their trade were known to both girls, with the risks of pregnancy, violence, and of course an assortment of diseases. Susan and her sister were always watching for the Police when dealing with their clients, and they adopted their own little ways of trying to avoid arrest. Policemen in Garrison towns like Plymouth were able to arrest prostitutes, arrange medical examinations and, if they had a disease, they were detained in a hospital for sometimes up to three months. This was something they were both keen to avoid. Eventually they were able to find the lodgings they currently lived at in Lower

Lane. This did though at one time involve having to provide sexual favours to their landlord to keep the accommodation; he would threaten to evict them if they didn't. This was no hardship to Susan and her sister as, due to his age and heavy drinking; they were easily able to deal with his fumbled advances and his inability to attempt intercourse. He was well known locally in business, and to put an end to his constant harassment, a threat about exposing his lack of ability to a few indiscreet locals was the answer for Susan. He didn't attempt to touch them again, but they knew they were on rocky ground with him and made sure they paid the rent on time.

Susan's sister eventually married a naval seaman she had met in the Napoleon Inn, but continued to live in Lower Lane, occupying rooms next to Susan's. She gave up working the streets following the birth of her daughter, as she now received steady support. Her husband was of course away a lot at sea and she still tended to visit many of the ale houses in the area, enjoying the company of men, but warding off their advances. Susan sat on the rocks after bathing, staring at the sea and thinking about wanting change in her life, at the moment, this could only remain a constant dream. She did not know how her life could be changed, and she wondered what the days ahead would bring.

Chapter 4

One person who was desperate to move to Plymouth to find work spent most days planning his next move. During the early summer days of 1874 Henry Kitts an itinerant labourer managed to find farm work on the edge of Dartmoor, about ten miles North of Plymouth. He had been lucky with work over the past few months but to his credit had proved his worth to any willing employer, providing them with a strong hard worker who kept himself to himself. Conversation was something that didn't come easy to Henry but he had learnt, from listening to others, that there was work to be had in Plymouth - particularly with the development of the railway. He made up his mind that he would eventually head in that direction, but he must first find more work in order to save money. Money was a necessity to enable him to support himself whilst initially looking for work when he reached Plymouth. Food and places to sleep would require money; not like the life he had been used to in the country, where food and a place to sleep came with his farm work. Thinking more than talking was the one thing Henry did do a lot of. His mind was always racing with ideas about the future and the better chances he could have. Most nights, before putting his head down to sleep, he would lay there dreaming about making the move but, inevitably, these thoughts were interrupted by thoughts of the past. These were thoughts he couldn't block out, no matter how hard he tried, but he knew his life must change.

Henry had been drifting around either side of the Devon and Cornwall borders since leaving home, but he was never able to settle for long in one place.

Little was known about him, even by those work colleagues he came into contact with, but that was how he preferred it. He would make a point of doing his normal thing, avoiding conversation. People he met referred to him as 'the quiet one'. If the subject of his background came up he told everyone he had been brought up on a farm and his parents were dead.

In his quiet moments a lot of his thoughts were about his lack of ability to converse; it bothered him and he wished he could be more outgoing. He knew he had to change to get accepted and ultimately seek new employment, but his past had not required him to talk much and he had rarely seen many other people in his early years.

At times Henry even thought to himself that he could remember little about his poor hard upbringing or was it a case of not wanting to remember it. He could certainly remember his violent father and the regular beatings he received from his hands. The violence could happen at any time, with the slightest upset triggering outbreaks. Henry had learnt as he got older to avoid them by keeping his distance, taking care not to say or do the wrong thing in his father's presence. The lack of a mother who died in childbirth had also given him little or no contact with women, and he was aware that he was a bit in awe of them, not knowing what to say or how to act when he initially met one.

The life with his father in the farm cottage several miles outside Okehampton was lonely and meagre. The badly run-down cottage, which in winter was cold despite an open fire had broken windows and the thatch leaked. Repair of the cottage was a low priority to the farmer who, if any complaints were made, would always be keen to remind his father that it was rent free.

Henry's days were spent helping his father. There was little time for any form of education, with only occasional visits to school and, as a result, there was very little contact with other children. The visits from the authorities in the end seemed to come to nothing. They would just give up as he would always be working in the fields or hidden by his father when they attended.

From his hiding places Henry had several times heard his father tell the school authorities that he had left home and, to himself, Henry had thought that before long this would be true.

The land-owning farmer had taken him on as a labourer, but things got no better and he felt that he had endured enough of that life. He had been thinking about this for some time - putting away a small amount of money that he hid in the barn - and spending his time alone planning how and when he would leave, and what he would do. He decided early one morning that now the time was right, with nothing to lose and no feelings of loyalty or respect for his father.

His father had gone early that day to assist with cattle, leaving him to work in the fields. He watched his father walk away and quickly bundled his few clothes in a tied cloth, hurriedly making his way across the fields, and away from where he knew his father would be, walking in the direction of Tavistock. He kept glancing back towards the farm expecting to hear a shout but keeping close to the hedges so he wouldn't be noticed. It was a fine morning and Henry felt a chill in his body. He couldn't quite make up his mind if that was down to the early start or his anticipation of what he was doing and what was about to happen. He shrugged it off thinking to himself that it must be the latter as he was used to being up and about this early.

He kept walking, but it felt strange, and he kept thinking 'had he done the right thing' but was quickly able to convince himself it was and the small amount of money would initially provide for him until he found work.

The first nights away he slept wherever he could find shelter - in barns or woods - leaving early in the mornings. Whenever he could he used his dwindling money for food, mainly bread which he bought when visiting farms looking for work.

Henry managed to find the occasional casual farm labouring work to support him, along with general labouring and any part time work he could get. Harvest time was always good for work and he was found to be a willing worker, using his skills to cut corn by hand. A place to sleep in the barn and meals were also provided and this was his favourite work, but the needs for his skills were short.

He felt grateful for any work, as he avoided trouble, and kept himself free from the need to steal which he knew would happen if he did not have money. He had found the need on several occasions, though considered himself lucky not to be caught, but coming close on several occasions. It was only his ability to run fast that had saved him.

Henry knew that he must be getting closer to Plymouth and it was early evening when he knocked on the door of the farm owned by Horace and Mary Cooper. The farm had been in the family for many years, and they both worked hard looking after their animals and fields. Horace was sixty-three and Mary was fifteen years younger. Their marriage had been without doubt arranged by her parents, who were tenant farmers and a friend of Horace. He was in their opinion someone who would make a good husband and an ideal man for their daughter to marry. She was encouraged by them and eventually married him, settling into the life of being a farmer's wife. Mary and Horace became a good team working the farm but Mary found that her life was one continual daily routine. She rarely saw anybody other than the labourers they employed. Horace was a kind man but never showed much affection towards her, expecting her to carry out her daily tasks, including preparing his meals. Mary had resigned herself to the fact that this was how her life was going to be. They had no children; for whatever reason Mary never became pregnant and she now of course had to accept the fact that now it would never be different.

Kitts knocking on their door that day solved a decision they had been discussing for a while. Their problem was fixed. Their search for a worker had been fruitful.

Extra help was needed now, particularly as Horace was finding the work more tiring and difficult; he wanted to go easier with the heavy manual work, his hands were gnarled and not giving him the service, they used to. Following the departure of their labourer who had left to join the army they had used local casual labour, but often found that it was not available when they needed it, and not at all reliable.

The offer of work for Kitts, with a bed in a small rear stone shelter and meals, was more than he could have dreamed of, but he knew and did not want to tell them that he had no intention of staying permanently. His willingness to work though soon found favour with the Coopers. The farm was isolated, but the long days and hard work gave Kitts little time to worry about anything else, and he found he could save by not spending the money he earned.

Mary and Kitts spent most days together, working the fields, and milking the cows. At first, she found that it was difficult to get him to talk too much about anything. She was an outgoing person who conversed naturally and, gradually as he got to know her, he found that he opened up more and eventually told her all about his childhood. Mary had been careful not to push him too much but had gently encouraged him and she gradually saw some improvement. She used to think to herself, "I'll make him tell me everything before long".

What he had told Mary explained a lot about his natural quietness and it was obvious from the way he acted initially towards her that he found it awkward being in the company of women.

Mary knew that he had a long way to go to conquer his shyness, and used to say to him, "Henry, you have to stand up for yourself and make a life, nobody will give it to you, don't be afraid to use your tongue".

He used to laugh at this, but secretly he had a fondness for Mary; the way she treated him made him feel the way a mother would have. He didn't of course know any of this from personal experience but guessed this would be what it was like. Henry had respect for this lady and valued very much the things she said to guide him and try to make him a more confident man.

This was something he had never experienced in his life, someone taking an interest in him.

He knew also that he would be leaving here one day but knew he couldn't tell her. Henry Kitts wanted to make a new life and was ready for it. Both Mary and Horace were kind to him but were not to be part of his new life as he wanted it, once again his lack of ability to show any emotion took over; he would just have to forget them and move on.

Mary had a fondness for Kitts and felt sorry for him when she learnt about his background. She found something about him that she couldn't explain and used to spend time thinking about it whilst working. Maybe it was his vulnerability and lack of the normal men/women experiences of life.

Kitts and Mary had finished bringing the cattle into the barn and he had gone to his shelter, after washing under the courtyard pump, whilst she prepared supper. Horace had taken the horse and cart into the area North of Plymouth for a meeting with other farmers, which occurred about four times a year, when crops and other items were bought, sold and exchanged. He would be returning later that night no doubt, merry from consuming ale during his meeting. Kitts walked into the farmhouse kitchen and stood with his back to the fire watching Mary lay up the wooden table. He noticed she had changed out of her working clothes and thought to himself 'this was unusual'. She served the meal - which he ate quickly as he was hungry after his days' work. There was no initial conversation between them but he could feel her glancing at him, watching his face. This made him curious and he said, "Why do you keep looking at me Mary, you're making me nervous, have I done something wrong"

Mary smiled at him and said, "Isn't a lady allowed to admire a handsome face?"

He had never heard Mary speak like this to him before. It made his face redden and he said,' be off with you, I'm just your labourer".

Kitt finished his meal and Mary rose from the table - leaned over to lift his plate – and, as she did, she kissed him on top of his head. This startled Kitts and he jumped up, facing her, and said "Mary" but, before he had time to say anything further, she dropped the plate back on the table, pulled him towards her and quickly pressed her lips against his. She held him tightly against herself and her hand slipped down between his legs fondling him. Kitts was taken by surprise at the speed of this and pushed her away shouting "stop, why did you kiss and touch me that way?"

Mary let go of his shoulders and stood facing him smiling. She asked, "Why don't you like it, I can show you how?"

Kitts didn't know what to do and stood there staring at her totally confused.

Mary moved towards him and said, "Look, don't pretend you didn't like it, kiss me."

Kitts said "I can't - look I don't want to hurt you, I work for you, I like and respect you, but I don't have those sorts of feelings for you".

Mary was taken back by his remarks and looked down at the floor thinking to herself how she had misjudged the situation and had gone too far. With tears welling up, she shook her head and said, "I don't know what came over me, I've made a fool of myself. I've grown fond of you Henry and just got carried away, it was a stupid thing to do to you but please understand how lonely my loveless life is."

Kitts looked at Mary, feeling some pity for her. Reaching out he caught hold of her hand and said "Mary, I have so much to thank you for. You have helped me to gain some respect and confidence and I will never forget that."

Mary squeezed his hand and said "I plead you not to say anything to Horace it was just me, a silly old woman, behaving badly. You must understand I have no love in my life Horace is a good man but he doesn't understand a woman needs some loving care."

Kitts stood silent - staring at the floor for what seemed ages to Mary - eventually looking up at her he released her hand and said "No I won't say anything, you have been good to me." I am off to my shelter though now, I think that's best and all can be forgotten." Mary nodded and started clearing the table. She felt stupid and wished she had not let her feelings show in that way at all.

Kitts walked to his shelter, so confused. He undressed and lay down thinking about what had happened. It had taken him by surprise, but he was not upset at all. He couldn't tell Mary but, now that he had time to think about it, he had actually enjoyed the kiss. He also thought to himself that he had handled the situation well, and that was in no small part to Mary and the time she had spent with him building his confidence. He fell asleep grinning and thinking to himself that his first kiss had been with a 48-year-old woman. This was something he would definitely, always, have to keep to himself.

The next morning Kitts thought about the previous night but his main thought was focussed on him leaving and going on his way to Plymouth; it was decided, he would leave after the harvest. They were both very quiet as they worked and no mention was made of the previous night as they dealt with the cattle. They avoided eye contact and their conversation during the day was limited to working matters. The next few weeks they found that their relationship had gradually returned to as it was, and nothing was ever said again.

The harvest was completed on time, with the weather providing just the right conditions for the work. The long days finished with a hearty meal, and ale, followed by a deep sleep – all ready and eager to start early the next day.

It was October 1874; Kitts waited until he could see that the Coopers had turned in for the night. He prepared his belongings, wrapped them in a cloth and collected his money from behind a stone in the wall of his shelter. He crept around the back wall of his shelter, purposely keeping away from the dogs chained at the front of the house and hoping not to make any noise. Close to his shelter was the stone wall of Lower Field, he carefully climbed over this dropping his belongings on the other side. There was a full moon which made it easier to cross the field and he made his way off their land to the lanes.

Kitts did feel guilty about leaving, and that same chill he had experienced when he left home came over him again; at one stage he stopped and almost turned back, but he knew he wanted a new full life and to achieve this he knew he must forget other people and follow his dream. The Coopers were kind but now that part of his life must be left behind.

Reaching the lane made his journey easier. He had time on his side and some bread he had packed to ease any hunger.

He walked for several hours, keeping to the lanes leading to the highway into Plymouth. Resting every few miles Kitts found some water in a cattle trough in a field beside the lane. He had enough money to find lodgings for a while when he reached his destination. He'd started to feel the excitement.

Kitts stopped at a tavern North of Plymouth, ate a hearty meal but decided not to stay the night as this would save him some money. He climbed a stone wall, entered some woods, and found a place to sleep. The night was fine, there was a little chill in the air, but he was used to the open air and he settled down for the night thinking about his next day, and hopefully how his life would change.

Chapter 5

Kitts rose early from his woodland sleep. It had been dark when he arrived at the woods, and he had walked and stumbled what he thought was far enough away from the highway to conceal himself. He blinked, stretched his arms but had difficulty immediately thinking where he was. His eyes gradually accustomed themselves to the dawn light; he shivered in the chilled early morning air as he brushed dried leaves and patches of mud from his clothes. He stood looking around, trying to get his bearings, and acclimatise himself to the surroundings. He could hear the sound of water and remembered he had heard water running when he first arrived. He walked in that direction, finding a small gulley with water running off from the moorland. He bent down filled his hands with icy water, swilling it around his face causing him to screw his eyes up as the coldness hit him. He scooped up several more handfuls which he quickly drank, wiping his mouth with the back of his hand. Fortunately, he did not feel hungry after his meal at the tavern the previous night and decided he would try and last until he reached the town. He gathered his belongings together and made his way back to the highway, weaving his way through the undergrowth and small branches which accounted for him stumbling the previous night. He approached the boundary wall, looked over - seeing the road and checking in both directions - before slowly jumping down on to the road. He checked the direction and started walking towards what he hoped would be Plymouth.

After walking for several hours Kitts was relieved when buildings and some people started to appear. He noticed that nobody was looking at him, or taking any particular notice of him, they were all going about their lives. He obviously did not look out of place and suddenly thought to himself 'why should I'; many others must have undertaken the same journey from the country seeking work. This boosted his confidence and he pulled himself upright; he had been worried about the change. After all, he had only been used to the country and had very little contact with strangers. He had also been wondering how people would react towards him and, as he walked, he smiled to himself thinking 'I must remember what Mary told me and use my tongue'.

Kitts started to notice that he was now walking down streets lined with houses either side and he was instantly struck by the size of the buildings and the number of people; he hadn't ever seen so many people in one place. Horse and carts were numerous, carrying goods; this was certainly all new to him. He kept looking around in amazement, colliding with a man walking towards him; he stumbled and the man grabbed hold of his arm, preventing him from falling, and said, "Sorry my son, you alright, I was trying to dodge you but you was looking up and walking towards me. I couldn't get out your way in time".

Kitts, feeling a bit sheepish, looked at the man and said "Yes, my fault I've not been 'ere before. This is Plymouth isn't it? I was looking to see how I find the railway being built, I'm looking for work".

The man said "yes, the best thing for you to do is keep walking this road until it don't go on no further, you can then ask again."

Kitts nodded at the man and continued walking, eventually finding himself surrounded by larger buildings and turnings going off both ways and thought 'this must be where the man meant.'

He was hungry by now, and looked both ways up and down the street, being pleased when he saw a tavern.

He went in and was immediately surprised by the noise and the number of people either stood or sat drinking. Nobody took any notice of him and he pushed his way to the bar, looked towards a woman who was serving and said "I want some ale, and can I get some food?"

The woman behind the bar looked up at him and said, 'You wait your turn I'll get to you, we have some beef and potatoes, that's all my love."

Kitts felt himself go red, and kept looking straight ahead, not wanting to see if anyone was looking at him. She finished serving, poured some ale which she put in front of him on the counter. "Will the beef do you" she said?

Kitts thought 'anything will do' and nodded, waiting whilst she went and got his food; he paid and said, "Do you know where the railway is being built, I'm looking for work?"

She said, '" You ought to go and ask that lot sat by the pillar - they all work there I think, they's always in here drinking and talking 'bout their work'."

Kitts still didn't look straight at her and said, "I'm new to this town - can you tell me where I am"?

He knew as soon as he said it that it was a stupid question and was even more embarrassed when she and several others stood near him burst out laughing and said, "You'm in the Old

Guildhall Tavern in Whimple Street me love, the finest place in town, now you enjoy your beef".

Kitts was embarrassed but sat at a table and decided to eat his food first before talking to the men but kept his eye on the group whilst he did. He finished, scraped his plate to get the last mouthful stood, and pulled himself to his full height. He took a deep breath and told himself to be confident, walking to the table with the men. As he approached, one of the group looked up at him and said "Are you joining us for a drink?"

Kitts was surprised by the way the man spoke, he had not heard anyone speak that way before – he could understand him but it was a strange accent, they must be from another country he thought. He looked down at the man and said "I was told you work on the railway, I'm looking for some work if there is any, I can give a good day anytime."

The same man said "Ah if its work you be looking for you need to speak to Mr Relph, he's in charge, our boss man; tell you what, you find yourself at the railway tomorrow at six, and he'll be there then to speak to. Are you going have that drink then?"

Kitts said "Thanks, no I won't, I need some rest I've been travelling all day, but how do I find it."

The man smiled looked at his group and said "Oh, just as we did when we came from Ireland."

Kitts nodded at the man, and walked away puzzled and thinking 'well, that explains why they talk like that, but they seemed friendly enough', but he didn't really know where Ireland was. He might ask them if he saw them again.

He managed to get a room upstairs for the night and took his belongings up. He found it was more comfortable than what he had been used to in the shelter and fell asleep easily - tired from his journey.

Rising early the next day was not a problem, and he was directed to the railway workings, where he found Mr Relph - a contractor for the London and South-Western Railway. The railway system was undergoing development within the City and also linking towns in the local counties. There was plenty of work for those prepared to show willing and reliability. Kitts was a strong looking individual and was taken on as a navvy, starting work the next day.

He returned to the Tavern and was pleased to get lodgings in an attic room, which reduced the cost.

The work on the railway was hard, most days were spent digging sections for track laying and shifting stones to provide ballast for the tracks. He considered himself lucky as, with the development of the railways, this was a steady job with regular money and he started to feel perhaps he had a better future. He had even bought new clothes.

Kitts soon settled in to the routine of long days but enjoyed the work none the less.

When he had money, he started to enjoy a drink, and this became his routine on most evenings. He used the downstairs bar, sitting alone, but deciding - as he reflected on his life - that he must get out and explore the area more. Several of the other locals had got to recognise him and greet him, and he liked this feeling part of the establishment.

During his working time, he had been befriended by several of the Irish labourers who worked alongside him on the line construction gang, including several he had seen in the Tavern when he first arrived. Their friendly nature and acceptance of him, mixed with their banter, started to ease his reluctance to mix and make friends. This was all completely new to him, nobody had treated him in this way before, and he began to feel almost as an equal to them.

Gradually without him realising his confidence increased. He also tried to remember Mary's advice; he conversed more easily, and even joined the other workers on pay days for a drink, though he found he could not match their ability in consumption. He had on several occasions tried, resulting in him staggering to his lodgings, oversleeping, and almost being late for work the next day.

Chapter 6

Kitts made the decision to explore the local area now that he felt more confident and accepted, he visited the High street on several occasions. This being close to his lodgings, he soon found more life and importantly, a choice of ale houses. He in turn visited all of them but had increasingly become fond of the Napoleon Inn. He could sit alone and nobody bothered him, other than a few locals who often greeted him when he came in. He almost began to feel like a regular and liked the feeling of being recognised and accepted. There was no doubt in his own mind that, since he started work on the railways and mixed with colleagues both at work and socially, his whole outlook and approach to life was different. He felt at ease when people spoke to him and was able to converse, though he knew that he was still not confident talking with women. He had not come into contact with them much, but he hoped this would change, as he realised he had the feelings and needs of any normal man.

Susan Foster was on the prowl looking for business and had spotted Henry Kitts, though not for the first time, amongst the regular drinkers at the Napoleon Inn. She noticed that his manner was somehow different to her normal noisy drunken clients, and in that respect; she could certainly speak from experience. He caught her eye and she liked the look of him, he was swarthy, rugged and clean looking; someone who worked outside she thought to herself. He dressed as if he was a workman, wearing his moleskin trousers, white shirt and black unbuttoned waistcoat. More importantly, she thought to herself, he also looked like he earned a wage and that alone may be good. As she stood near the bar surveying the room for business she had caught sight of his occasional furtive glances towards her. She remembered he had been sat in that seat before, but she had never spoken to him, nor had he made any approach to her. She had never seen him with anyone, but had seen him occasionally acknowledging a few other regulars, he was a quiet one alright she thought.

She had met men who acted this way before; they were shy with women, and she had recognised that for some it may be their first time of going or wanting to go with a woman. That had made her feel in control and tended to relieve what to her had become a ritual and, at times desperation to make money to survive.

Looking around the bar she could not see any likely punters and decided to approach Kitts - sitting opposite him on a stool; he might buy her a drink at least she thought.

She stared directly at his face, smiling at him, and noticed he was looking nervous and blushing. Before she could say anything, he blurted out "Sorry I was staring, I was trying to see who you were looking for, and I've noticed you in ere before." She said "Well bless you darling, I'm Susan Foster and part of the building"; She fluttered her eyes towards him and said "ave you some coins? Cause - if so - you can ave some fun with me."

He said "Sorry must be a no, I'm just aving a drink on me own, didn't mean to be…… "

She burst out laughing and reached across the table cupping the back of his head with her right hand; "Bloody ell you'm a strange one, ave you never ad a woman? Don't be shy I'll show you what to do, then you'll know for next time, ha ha."

He pulled his head away from her hand and said "Look no, not this time I'll……."

She said, "You'll what? Oh, forget it; ok lovie buy me a drink, you make me laugh, I need money so can't hang around - ave work to do - what's yer name by the way?"

"Henry, - Henry Kitts"

Kitts felt angry with himself that he had no experience with women and his natural shyness had made him look a fool; she was laughing at him he thought. He now knew what she was but, for some reason, felt a certain immediate liking for her. He could not describe her as good looking, she was older than him, had let herself go, but her personality, confidence, and openness towards him was everything he was not but wanted to be. He had to admit to himself that she had instantly made him feel good and wished he had the courage to go with her; it would be his first time. He got their drinks from the bar and returned to the table.

Foster thought as she watched him at the bar, and whilst sipping their ale, that she liked his innocence and felt in some way he was a challenge. He was certainly different and she noticed how he sat in silence looking down and making only short replies to her conversation. She could not help but also notice the way he was looking at her. She must be getting soft she thought to herself, he's only another man. She drank the remains of her ale quickly, rose, and smiled at Kitts saying "You make sure you come and see me 'Enry, I'll give you a good time."

Kitts smiled nervously and watched her as she moved away.

She knew they would meet again; she would make sure of that somehow.

Susan pushed her way through the crowd and Kitts saw her stop and speak with a crowd of men near the bar; he saw her laughing and suddenly leave with a man, who had his arm around her waist. To his surprise this made him feel angrier than ever with himself for not being bolder. He had missed his chance to be with her, she was going off with someone else. He did not understand why he was feeling like this.

He didn't know what made him do it but he suddenly got up and followed the pair of them outside. He kept his distance and watched as they disappeared around a corner into a lane and darkness. He took a few steps into the lane and stopped, waiting and listening. Her laughing voice and the man's grunting noises left him in no doubt what was happening. He turned and hurried out of the lane back towards his lodgings. As he walked quickly along the streets he ignored everyone and everything, he was feeling a strange mix of emotions, anger at himself and Jealousy. Why was he angry at seeing her with another man? He knew what she did and he had only just spoken to her? He couldn't understand why he was feeling this way he had just met her yet felt obsessive; he decided he didn't want any other men touching her, but that was ridiculous.

He returned to his lodgings and, after undressing, lay on his bed finding he couldn't sleep. Kitts couldn't get the thoughts of this woman out of his head, but also remembering that the fumbled kiss that Mary had given him was his only experience of a woman. He thought about meeting her and listening to her speak, yes if he was honest she had let herself go, but underneath it all he felt there was something, he could change her and give her a better life. He must try to see her again, and not be so shy and slow to move. The thoughts were gradually overtaken by sleep, and by the following morning he decided he was being stupid and the drink had addled his mind. She was a prostitute and would not be interested in him other than for money, he must forget the woman

Kitts spent the next few days immersed in his work, putting any thoughts of her to the back of his mind and, during the evenings, he avoided the area of the Napoleon contenting himself with a drink in the bar below his lodgings, or close by.

The next pay day, after completion of his days' work, Kitts joined some of his Irish work mates drinking in an ale house close to the railway, near where they worked. He had drunk more than normal and when he left them he felt good but there was a slight stagger in his walk.

He did not know what led to him walking towards the Napoleon but he didn't care, he was happy - something was driving him. It was raining and he smiled to himself as he kicked his work boots into the puddles that dotted the streets, causing the rainwater to splash up over him. He was being directed by a strange but good feeling that had built up inside him again. He felt just like he did when she first spoke to him. Something had crossed his mind several times since that first meet, and now he wanted to laugh out loud; what was she called, he hadn't even asked for her name, she had told him and he was pretty sure it was Susan, but he couldn't recall anything else.

Business for Susan this night was non-existent. She had visited several of the ale houses and walked around the Barbican area. She thought it must be the rain, and also knew that most of the fishing boats were at sea.

When she first arrived on the Barbican she walked towards a group of people stood near the water's edge. There was a lot of shouting and arm waving, and when she reached them she saw a man lying on the quayside surrounded by the group of men. She listened to them talking and heard that they had pulled him from the water, she moved closer looking at the body, she could see the face had a strange colour but she did not recognise him. One of the men said, 'I don't know his proper name, its him though he's Fishy Mick he sometimes works the boats, I saw he was very drunk earlier, he must have fallen in the tide, don't look like he got any cuts or anything'. The group of men agreed it was him, and one of them volunteered to go and get the Police. The secret that Fishy Mick was going to use to his own advantage had now died with him, and luck was on the side of the thief.

The finding of the body and the man's identity meant nothing to Susan; she didn't know the man, it didn't bother her and she had seen dead bodies before, and besides the Police would be around soon, she needed to move away. She didn't want to be there with a body when the Police came, they might try and involve her.

She pulled her ragged cape around herself providing her with some protection against the driving rain. She was tired, wet, depressed, and without money again. Her life was a mess and she only had herself to blame. Emotions that she had not experienced before were surfacing; she had cried herself to sleep a lot recently and had even contemplated ending her miserable existence. She had thought several times about the man 'Enry' she had met in the Napoleon - what was it about him - he was just another man. This was right but, most she met took advantage of her, he didn't, he seemed shy. She walked in the direction of the High Street, it seemed to be darker than normal she thought, or was it her imagination. Susan took care on the Barbican cobbles as they were slippery and, as she glanced ahead, she could see a shadowy figure coming towards her. By its size, she could tell the figure was obviously a man. He was staggering slightly and looked sort of threatening to her. Her heart pounded slightly at first and she crossed away from the figure, hoping that she could avoid any contact by creating a gap between them. Only women like her would be on the streets at this time. She wanted to return home and avoid any sort of confrontation; her day was over, she needed sleep, she was not interested in bartering for business.

As she got adjacent to the figure she looked away towards a shop window to avoid eye contact and heard a softly spoken but slightly slurred man's voice say "Hello again, do you remember me, I was looking for you."

This made Susan stop; she looked up towards the figure and sighed with relief, recognising him from the Napoleon.

She said "Bloody hell 'Enry its you from the other night, you frightened me for a minute, what's wrong with me, I thought you'd forgotten me?"

Kitts shook his head and had no control over the mysterious force driving his actions; as he softly touched her face, her scary emotions turned to tears.

Susan was not sure herself about her tears; it was a mix of relief and the release of the tension she had been feeling. Why was she crying and yet be so pleased to see him?

He held her tight as she wept, he couldn't understand her tears.

As they mixed with the rain on her face, he said nothing, not knowing what to say anyway. All this was new and strange to him, but whatever was happening made him feel warm inside. There was no conversation between them; there was no need, they were being driven by instinct and she just looked up at his face and smiled. Susan took his arm, wiped her face with the back of her hand and led him up the High Street to her room, holding tightly on to him. Kitts did not protest he let her lead him; he would not let her slip away this time. As they entered Lower Lane Susan saw a Policeman making his way towards them down High Street with another man. She was pleased he had not seen her and they were close to her room.

Once in the room Susan pulled off Kitts wet clothes; he made no protests and she then undressed herself, Kitts trying not to stare at her naked body as she pulled him towards the bed.

Kitts had never spent time alone like this with a woman; they sat on the bed holding each other and talking, their clothes drying by the fire – both of them wrapped in the same blanket. He realised he was telling her things that he would not have had the courage to do before, but it seemed so natural, his inhibitions had disappeared. They held on to each other tightly until Susan pulled him towards her as she lay on her back, and Kitts soon found out what he had been missing for so long. Exhausted he lay on his back breathless and holding tightly on to Susan. They soon fell into a deep sleep.

Chapter 7

Kitts woke early the next morning. As his head cleared he started to come to his senses; he couldn't immediately work out where he was - it wasn't his lodgings. He stretched and his arm touched something in the bed which at first startled him; he suddenly remembered and smiled to himself as the memories of his first night with a woman came back to him. He slowly sat up and just stared towards her face He got carefully out of bed and saw that Susan was still curled up asleep - creeping around he tried his best not to wake her. He dressed in his dry clothes, looking over at her as he put the clothes on, all the time smiling to himself as he thought about the previous night. Looking around the room, Kitts found some stale bread which he ate quickly. He washed the bread down with some water, which was warm but quenched his thirst.

He carefully opened the door which squeaked, causing him to open it in small movements. He smiled as he took one last look towards Susan before he left. The front door opened easily. There was a dead seagull on the step which he pushed away with his foot into the side corner of the step - near the house wall. He crept into the street, feeling the cold early morning air on his face. He was happy and walked quickly, reliving the previous night as he made his way to the railway; he was not sure what would happen between them. He knew what Susan did and the thought of this made him angry and jealous, but he did not know how she felt, and if he would see her again in the same way. If she didn't want him in his way he would have nothing to do with her; he was not going to pay her for services. These thoughts kept returning to his mind throughout the day, repeating them over and over again. He thought 'what shall I do.'

The day seemed long, and he couldn't wait to finish work. He shovelled ballast and, again wondered about Susan and what would happen next. The meeting and the night spent together had all happened so fast. This was all new to him, he was surprised, pleased, and totally confused at the same time; all these mixed thoughts ran through his mind as he worked. He was glad to finish work and, despite everyone's protestations, turned down the chance to enjoy a drink with the rest of his gang. His mind was in a turmoil over this lady and he walked slowly back to his room, where he lay on his bed and thought about what happened. These feelings were all strange to him but there was no doubting how good he felt and, more than ever, Kitts knew he had to see her again. Oh yes, he definitely wanted to see her again, but was worried that she wouldn't want him. How would he deal with that? He decided that the only way was to take the bull by the horns; he would eat and then go looking for her, starting with her house.

Susan was angry when she found Kitts missing; he hadn't woken her to say he was leaving. Obviously, this man had used her just like all the others. She'd been wrong about him – every man treated her same and this bastard hadn't paid either. She needed money to live and spent most of the day in her room thinking about Henry; should I forget him - what was the attraction - did he feel the same? All these thoughts whizzed around in her head. He though was very naïve about women – vulnerable, and she liked this. It kept crossing Susan's mind that she was getting soft. She should just forget this man and tell herself again that they were all the same. She knew though deep down that Kitts was different and he had something which had attracted her and drawn her to him. From the first time she had seen him in the Napoleon this woman could not get Kitts out of her mind. With all the doubts she had she knew this meeting was special and made up her mind that the only way to know the answer was to find Henry and have it out with him. She was relieved he had told her where he was staying.

Kitts was half way through his meal when he heard a voice behind him say, 'You are alive then you beggar, you left without speaking"

He spun around in his chair, recognising at once the sound of Susan's voice. Jumping up, he threw his arms around her neck, and blurted out "Oh I didn't want to wake you and I didn't know if you wanted to see me again either. I hate what you do, I can't think about you being with other men – you mustn't do it".

Susan said "I hate it to. I want to change, but I can't give it up, I need money to survive. You must understand it's all I have, there's no other work for me, I have no other way of surviving, and I've tried."

Kitts let her go - staring hard into her eyes and said "I don't know what to say to you Susan, it kills me to see you go off like you do with other men and I can't be with you if you carry on going with other men. I want you to stop."

Susan said "you want me to stop just like that, you was only with me a night; you don't own me, you've only just met me and no man controls me. Tell me Henry what am I supposed to do for money?"

Kitts said "I just can't bear the thought of you being touched by other men, you got to stop for me."

Tears began to well up in her eyes; she turned and ran to the door shouting "sorry, sorry, you're just like the rest, you just want to use me, you want me to stop, but how can I, and how am I to live."

Kitts stood wondering what to do next; he went to the door but there was no sign of her, she had disappeared into the lanes. He must find her he thought; he had upset her, he hadn't explained things well. He knew only too well he was no good at expressing his feelings, and what a complete mess he'd made of trying to explain. He must tell her he would look after her and provide for her if she would give up this daily work. He hurried from the bar.

Chapter 8

Susan ran into the street, brushing away tears with the back of her hand; she didn't care where she was running, and couldn't understand why she was acting in this way - what was so different with this man? She hurried down a side lane, suddenly remembering it was a dead end, but sat down on the ground at the end, burying her head in her hands and sobbing. He doesn't want me like I am, so he can go to hell along with rest she thought. I'll get by without him. He's just a using bastard. I need money to live, I can't just give up because he says so and don't like me doing it. Her thoughts were interrupted by the sudden sound of heavy footsteps coming towards her; Susan froze, looked up frightened and her heart was pounding; it was dark, there was no light she couldn't see who was coming and there was no escape behind her. 'I'll fight for me life if I ave to she thought and jumped up shouting out, "who's there, get away from me" At the same time she ran quickly towards the footsteps - with her head down and coming to a sudden stop - as she ran into a large figure, nearly causing both of them to fall. Strong arms grabbed hold of her and a voice said "Hold it there, what are you up to - its PC Bennett - stop struggling and stay where you are."

Panting she said "Oh bloody ell, you scared me to death, I thought me end had come; I aint done nothing, I was just upset over a bloody man and went down the lane to think and get away."

" I saw you go down the lane Foster and came to see what no good you were up to; you get back home and do yer thinking there. I shall look to see if there's anything wrong, and if so I know where to find you - be on your way now."

"Honest, I aint done nothin, you will see I'm telling the truth honest mister policeman."

Susan hurried back out of the lane, still panting, but was relieved it was him and not someone who had seen her go down the lane, following her and wanting to attack her or something. That was the first time she was happy to see PC Bennett, he was normally one person she tried to avoid. She hurried away and did manage a smirk thinking 'I suppose they are useful sometimes, but her thoughts quickly returned to the present and that bastard Kitts.

She decided she needed a drink and to get away and clear her head from all thoughts of Kitts, walking to the Napoleon, where Adam served her ale. She decided she would forget Kitts. It was busy and the thought crossed her mind that there may be some business here; she needed money. Before long, a group of seamen came and stood in front of her, with one of them looking and smiling in her direction. She smiled and said "you looking for business my lover"

The seaman laughed, came closer to her, looking her up and down and said "I need a few drinks first, then I'll see if you look any prettier me old tart." His group burst out laughing and shouted "You'll need a lot more than a few then Sam."

Susan glowered at them, cursing them under her breath, and moved around them, nearer the bar, finding herself stood beside another group celebrating their catch and returning from sea. She would wait for one of them to catch her eye, and then she would move in.

Kitts walked into Whimple Street, looked up and down, but there was no sign of Susan. He hurried into High Street trying to remember where exactly she lived; he could remember it was a small lane and searched several that ran off the Street but could not be sure. Eventually he walked up Lower Lane and saw her front door; there was no doubt in his mind, because the seagull was still where he had pushed it. He banged on the door, but nobody bothered to answer, or wanted to. In High Street, a fruitless search of the bar of the Naval Reserve was followed by him taking a walk into the Napoleon. He saw Susan. She was stood with her back towards him and a man had his arm draped around her neck; they were both smiling and were in deep conversation, with their faces close to each other. He stood there for a while staring at them, feeling the anger building up inside him. He moved quickly towards them and grabbed the man from behind, pushing him to one side and onto the ground saying "let her go - don't touch her or you'll have me to deal with, do you 'ear me."

The man fell against a table spilling all the drinks as he tried to keep his balance and the bar suddenly went quiet. People turned to see what the shouting and noise was about. Kitts leaned over him with his right fist raised. When the man saw the size of him and the anger in his face, he waved his hand towards him indicating he wanted no trouble. He just rolled over and moved out of the way on the floor. Susan quickly moved towards Kitts, grabbed his arm and shouted, "Don't hit him you bloody idiot he aint done nothing." Kitts stared at Susan with wild looking eyes, caught hold of her arm and dragged her towards the door. She shouted "Get off me, you're hurting me you bastard." The Inn keeper was alerted by the disturbance, and moved towards them and shouted "Get out the pair of you" pushing them into the street. Kitts dragged Susan a few paces and said "I don't want you with other men. I want to look out for you." Susan was scared at the way he was acting; he had hurt her arm and had a strange look in his eyes. "Let go of me, you'm urtin me, you're like a mad dog. What's wrong with you?" She could see that his face was contorted with anger and his sudden outburst of violence had surprised and frightened her. He let go her arm, which she rubbed and decided to keep walking. Kitts followed a few paces behind her in silence. Neither of them saw PC Bennett, who had stepped back into a shop doorway to quietly observe the street. "I told you to go home earlier; I've seen enough of you tonight." The booming voice made both of them jump, and Susan didn't reply. She just waved her arm, pointing in the direction of Lower Lane and quickening her pace, not daring to look back to see Kitts. She was so relieved to reach the door of the house and see that he did not follow her. Hurrying in she closed the door of the room and climbed on the bed - her heart was pounding - and she was shaking. In all her time on the streets nobody had tried to stop Susan earning her living or control her. He was angry she thought, but what was it all about; why did he get like that, he knows what I do.

On seeing the policeman Kitts had decided to let her go and walk on, but he was not ready yet to go back to his lodgings. He walked around, angry at what he had seen; the sight of another man with his arm around Susan had incensed him. That's what had caused him to lose his temper and drag the man off. The night air with a slight breeze on his face made him start to think more rationally as he walked. He couldn't explain his actions. He realised he was jealous but he couldn't understand such emotions, they had taken over his every thought. He knew though that the only way to deal with this was to calm down. He needed to talk to her and explain that he wanted to be with her and would look after her; she wouldn't need to go with other men then, he could give her money.

Chapter 9

Kitts walked slowly into Lower Lane; he kept looking around - particularly for the policeman, as he didn't want to be seen by him again following the earlier warning. He stood outside Susan's door and, when he was happy that no one else was around, he banged loudly with his fist clenched at the same time shouting her name. He did this several times but nobody answered. His fourth knock was answered with a bucket of waste thrown down towards him from an upstairs window. This just missed him, and he was too late to see who had thrown it. Kitts cursed as he moved back out of the way, staring angrily up at the windows, searching for any movement. He decided then to wait opposite Susan's house; she had to come out some time, even if it meant him missing a day's work - though that wasn't a good idea, he needed the job. He sat on a step and watched the door. Fortunately, the previous day's rain had cleared and it was a mild night, but he found it difficult at times to keep his eyes open.

Susan had heard the door being banged and Kitts calling out her name but she wasn't going to answer. His actions towards her had frightened her; she had suffered violent men before during her street work, but nobody had ever acted in such a possessive way towards her. She couldn't understand it, they had only just met and he was demanding she gave up the street and not go with other men. He don't bloody own me she thought, I got to make money somehow to live.

She couldn't sleep, and spent a restless night turning from side to side thinking about Kitts and what had happened. She ran through the events time and time again but couldn't make any sense of them. She did think at one stage 'he is a handsome bastard though' but quickly put this thought out of her mind. His violence and temper worried her, and she shouldn't be thinking about his looks.

Susan then decided, after trying every way to get some sleep, to get up and go for a walk around the Barbican - the sea air would perhaps help to clear her mind.

She left the house quietly, keeping her head down, and didn't notice Kitts on the step opposite as she walked towards the High Street. He had seen her though and decided to let her walk some distance away from the house before approaching her so that she had no chance to run back in.

She nearly reached the end of Lower Lane when the sound of her name being called behind her made her shudder, stop suddenly, and turn - she knew that voice. She decided to continue walking. There would be other early risers around in the High Street; Kitts wouldn't touch her there she thought.

"Wait Susan, I want to talk to you; on me life I won't hurt you" Kitts shouted.

Susan turned towards him, but kept moving slowly backwards towards High Street. She shouted back at Kitts, saying "You bloody come near me and I'll holler murder, I swear I will." Kitts threw his hands in the air and said "I swear I won't touch you, its talking I want. If you go right out into the street - where we can be seen – you won't be frightened and you can listen to me." Hearing this gave Susan a little more confidence in her safety
and she bravely turned and walked into the centre of the High Street and stopped. "Ok talk, but so help me keep yer distance." Kitts stopped as well and said "I wronged you and acted jealous; I can't help it - I wants you and thought we could live together. I can provide for you and give you everything you need."
Susan burst out laughing. "Yer what" she said. "You expect me to believe you, I 'ardly knows you, and you thinks you owns me already."

Kitts looked down and said "How can I show you, give me a try you won't ave to work the streets any more I promise yer."
Susan said "I liked the look of you when I saw you first, but you frightened me in the Napoleon and you was wild; I don't know - how can we get along together? I likes the idea of giving up, but we just met. I never done this before and I can't think right as to whether I trusts you, you could 'urt me again "
Kitts said "Look I ave to get to the railway - I needs me job for money; I want to talk about us, you think on me and decide. I'll be in the Naval Reserve when I finishes, you come there, let me know. I swear I won't touch you."
Susan didn't reply. She stood and watched as he walked up the street, wondering if he meant what he said or is he just after me body for nothing. He hasn't had women before, why is he so smitten with me? This was a completely new situation for her; did he really mean it when he told her he wanted to be with her, or was it just because it was his first time and he couldn't get

over it; he had become besotted if he could be believed. Over the years because of what had happened to her Susan had built up a mistrust of men, seeing them only as a way to earn money. They both spent that day thinking about what had happened and wondering whether or not they would get together? Kitts knew he wanted to be with Susan and she liked him, but his temper worried and terrified her; she didn't know for sure if she would she be able to keep away from other men either and, not only that, did Kitts mean it when he said he would provide and always be there for her. All these unanswered questions were going through both their minds.

Kitts left work, walking slowly to his lodgings whilst trying to rehearse what to say to make Susan understand that he wanted to be with her. He knew that explaining himself was not his strong point, and he had to get it right to give him a chance of speaking to her again. As he walked he also thought how fast everything had happened since he came to Plymouth. He knew he was more confident in himself and was near to settling down, if she would have him and he could explain it right. He knew she was the first woman he had gone with, but for some reason he couldn't explain any of it or his feelings at all. It was such a mystery to him. Was this meant to be? He had felt smitten with Susan from when first setting his eyes her and knew from that moment he wanted to be with her. This was certainly an unexpected change in his life. It what was he wanted though and needed to make him happy; but Kitts knew that he must try and do his best to trust her.

Kitts returned to his lodgings, changed, left his room and walked to the Naval Reserve, sitting in the corner with his ale - a position where he could survey the room easily and see who came in thru the door. The bar was relatively quiet and, after having consumed three tankards, he began to feel edgy and started thinking that she wouldn't turn up and that she was probably with other men; what should he do, should he go looking for her?

He was staring at his drink thinking about going off to find her when his thoughts were suddenly interrupted. The door opened and Susan and another woman entered. They were both smiling. Susan looked towards Kitts and said "get us a drink then, you'm the one with the money."

The two women together made him feel edgy, and had caught him off balance. This was unexpected, and he wondered what they were up to. He went to the bar, bought three ales and returned to his seat, where the two were now sitting staring at him.

Susan, looking straight at him said "This is me sister Nancy, she lives in the next room to me and we looks out for each other. I've spoken about us to her and told her what 'appened, but she thinks if you can behave and provide, we ought to give it a try.

She says it will get me off the streets, caus' that's what she wants for me, she did it herself and is settled now."

Kitts felt a bit angry that she had spoken about him; he nodded towards her sister, who was looking sternly towards him. She said, as a warning "I don't know you yet but on me life I'll swing if you 'arms her - do you know what I'm saying. My sister don't need a violent man."

Kitts was taken a bit by surprise; he had rehearsed what he was going to say and had been thrown off his guard being confronted by the two of them.

He said "I was jealous, I like her a lot and, if she doesn't work the streets, it won't happen, I can provide for Susan. It is only her going with other men that makes me jealous. It won't happen if she stops, I earns' money to look after her."

The three sat in silence, all of them looking at the floor and wondering who was going to speak next. Suddenly, Nancy jumped up out of her seat, finished her ale, whispered something in her sister's ear, turned and left. She looked back towards Kitts as she walked away; it was a strange look, and he couldn't fathom what she was thinking.

He couldn't hear what she had said before leaving and turned to Susan to ask "what did she say?"

Susan smiled, looked him in the face and said "she thought you were ansome, so don't you go getting any ideas - if you'll does as you said you would, you can go and get your stuff and move into my room with me."

Kitts smiled at her, quickly slurped his ale caught hold of Susan's hand and led her out; at that moment he was a happy man, he knew that this is what he wanted, he could change her, she wouldn't have to sell her body to live.

Chapter 10

Kitts and Susan walked to his attic room above the Inn, gathered together his few belongings, paid for his room at the bar and then walked slowly outside -heading in the direction of Susan's room. Neither of them said anything, but they were both thinking hard and knew they would need to sort out their lives and it would need to be done from now. This was all going to be new for them. Various thoughts were going through their heads as they both tried to plan what they would say, and how it would affect them. Their silence was only interrupted with occasional looks and half smiles towards each other as they walked, but they both knew and could tell that their minds were racing. Once in Susan's room they silently sorted Kitts belongings, then sat on the bed facing each other, but both looking down - each of them wondering where to start, and what to say.

Susan was first to speak, she didn't look up but blurted out "You must give me regular money so I can put food on the table and pay the rent."

Kitts looked toward her and said "There must be no more other men; you mustn't work the streets, you know how jealous I am - if you do that I can provide."

Susan said "I does it to survive; if you do your bit I won't have to, I want to stop, I've 'ad enough of that life and its risks, I've been doin it too long, I'm sick of feeling used and abused'.

Kitts said, 'your face looks tired, I don't want you to have that life anymore'.

Kitts reached out, caught hold of Susan's hand and pulled her towards him resting his head on hers where they stayed for some time until they could no longer resist each other. The spark they had felt when they met was reignited, in no time they were both breathless and laid together with their arms entwined.

The next few weeks saw them both getting used to their new life. They spent every evening together, sometimes just sitting and talking and, when money allowed, having a drink in the Inns. Susan started taking pride in her room - scrubbing the floor and making sure their meagre belongings were tidy and there was always food for Kitts - mid morning and after his days' work. She also found that she felt better; her appearance had changed for the better. It had taken people that knew her some time to accept that the money she had was not stolen, and that she had settled down, but there were those who thought it wouldn't last, and were still suspicious of her.

Their daily routine continued for the first few months but gradually each of them noticed the old ways were returning. Kitts had started drinking with his workmates after work and would sometimes come home late and, at times, did not give her enough money, having spent it on drink. He in turn had noticed that Susan was sometimes not there when he arrived home; he could smell drink on her and started to wonder if she was back to her old ways - but she always had some excuse or little ploy to convince him otherwise.

All of these changes put thoughts in their heads about what may be happening and arguments started, with accusations being made to each other, mainly about drink, money, and men. There was little doubt that their life together was changing and drifting back to how they were before when they first met.

During some of their arguments Kitts had pushed Susan and raised his arm threatening to hit her, but her shouts about leaving had tended to defuse his anger and he had backed away without striking her.

It was April 1875 and they had been together for a few months, but the arguments had taken over their lives; Kitts was drinking heavily and Susan had been regularly visiting the Napoleon - gladly accepting free drinks and the company - but so far avoiding any physical contact with men, but had come near to it on several occasions.

She had threatened to leave Kitts during an argument about other men after he had struck her and blackened her eye and, the following afternoon, had sat in the room after consuming ale during the morning. Susan was now without money and had not been there when he came back for his mid-day meal.

Kitts came bursting angrily in through the door, seeing her sat on the floor in the corner.

"Where have you been, you were not here, there is no fire lit, I can smell drink?"

Susan didn't answer but looked at him with a semi smile on her face, at that moment not really caring.

Kitts lit the fire, turned towards Susan and said "where is my supper?"

"I have no money she replied; you drink it all away and leave me short."

"You have been with other men?" he asked in an accusing way.

"No if I had there would be money and you're pushing me that way."

Kitts thrust his hand in his pocket and took out coins which he slammed down on the table saying "You try it and I'll mark you, I try and do me best to provide a home, take the money now and get some supper."

Susan got up and walked towards the table, sweeping the coins away with her hand onto the floor shouting "You won't touch me, you were supposed and promised to provide; I ave kept my side and you just drinks it all. If you don't care for me I'll get money by using my old ways, I got to survive as well."

This remark incensed Kitts and he came towards her - pushing her in the back and causing her to fall on the floor. She rolled in a ball as he came quickly in front of her and felt several kicks connecting with her chest area; her arms were little defence from his heavy work boots. Susan tried to scream out "Stop it you bastard" but she lost consciousness from the searing pain and sudden difficulty in breathing before she could get the words out. Then there was nothing but blackness.

Susan awoke with a start the next day - a strange antiseptic smell in her nostrils - where was she? She stared around the room and, as her eyes slowly began to focus, she could see she was not in her own bed, and there were other beds in the room. A voice she didn't recognise said "Ah you're with us at last; you're in hospital, and you broke some ribs when you fell."

 Her eyes darted around the room, frantically thinking where was she and what was she doing there. When her mind began clearing, and she started to recall what had happened, she stared around frightened and bewildered wanting to scream out its all lies; a sudden pain in her chest though as she moved prevented her from trying to say anything at all. As Susan's eyes focussed she saw a nurse stood beside her and it gradually dawned on her where she must be; she didn't have a clue at all though how she had got there.

Her hands instinctively moved to her ribs and she could feel a dressing, but even the slightest movement caused extreme pain in her chest, so she did not continue examining her injuries. She raised her arms, which felt sore and saw that they were bruised along the sides. She had been to hospital before to be treated for minor injuries caused by fights and the occasional violent punter, but this was different, she suddenly felt scared and so alone.

The nurse said "you must rest" and before she could say anymore Susan interrupted, asking "ow did I get ere?"

The nurse told her it was a mystery to them all; and that a man had brought her to the hospital and left her with an orderly. "He wouldn't stop" she told Susan. "He just said he found you like this and carried you here. You rest now." Susan turned her head away, tears welling up in her eyes as she remembered

Kitts attack on her, all brought about by her threatening to go back to her old ways for money. He was obviously the man who had brought her; nobody else would have seen her, as it had all taken place in her room.

What would she do now? Her mind raced with many thoughts and, eventually, sleep took over. After a short time, she woke screaming, covered in sweat, the result of having bad dreams about what had happened. The nurse settled her down again but the thoughts returned. Kitts, unknown to Susan, had arrived at the hospital ward pleading to see her and hoping that nobody would recognise him but, by order of the doctor, she was not allowed visitors. He was allowed to stand at the entrance and look towards her bed for a few seconds and then told to go away and return the next day. Kitts was worried now, feeling so guilty about his violence. He had carried her to the hospital, but had left quickly - panicking about what would happen and what she would say. He had lost his temper once again over jealous thoughts and had taken it out on her in a moment of rage. He had though managed to avoid seeing her sister, and having to answer any awkward questions and wanted to keep it that way. He knew that it was now going to be over between them, but he wanted to be sure about what she had said. A word out of place could mean trouble for him and the loss of his work, this was his main concern.

Susan spent her time resting and thinking about her life. Her thoughts during this time had gone from one extreme to the other; should she have nothing more to do with him, or take him back? She knew others would not agree, particularly her sister, but she started to feel responsible for what had happened and blamed herself for saying she would go with other men. She had provoked Kitts; it was her own fault - she knew he was jealous of other men and she shouldn't have said it. She then thought I can't have any more violence though that will have to stop. These thoughts kept her awake but she decided she wanted him back, at least if they can go back to how they were she would have money. It was easier to take money off him than the punters if she kept her side, and she wouldn't have to work the streets. She decided she would lie about what happened - nobody else had seen it - he must not abuse her though. She then dismissed these thoughts as stupid, and didn't really know what she would do.

Kitts turned up at the hospital the next evening, walking slowly and gingerly towards Susan's bed, his head was bowed. He wasn't sure what to say, or what she would say, and just stared towards the bed not looking directly at her face.

"I hurt you in a moment of madness and jealousy, I don't expect you to forgive me, but I've calmed down and know I went too far. I thought you had been with other men and I'm sorry; just don't say anything to anybody about it, I'll leave you."

Kitts turned and walked away from her bed. He'd gone just a few paces when Susan said "Come back Enry, I want to speak about it, I provoked you about other men, I know you are jealous and you lost your temper over it, but you didn't ave to hurt me so much, you broke me ribs."

Kitts said "I shouldn't ave hurt you so much but I thinks you are with others, I can't control myself, it boils up inside me; ave you told anyone?"

Susan was feeling sore with the talking and the heavy breathing caused by her anxiety and said "No, but them wonders and keeps asking me." This was partly true, but she also wanted to keep him worried and see what he did and said; At least she was safe where she was.

Kitts said "Don't tell anyone - I'll be in trouble and lose me job and ave no money I'll move out, I know I deserves it, just don't say nothing."

Susan didn't reply. She just stared at him and thought, he's really only worried about his violence to me and people finding out and him losing his job; does he care at all about me and what he did?

She said "You go now, I can't talk much cause of the hurt, I'll think about what I want, you seem more worried about someone finding out than of me and what you done."

Kitts said "All I wanted is for us to have a proper home, I thinks you are with men, I drinks to stop the thoughts and then gets jealous; we fights and then I hurts you, but if I loses me work we have nothing."

Susan was confused then. She said "I'm tired, you come and see me again when I've ad time to sleep and think; just go, leave me alone."

Kitts looked at her but didn't reply; he half nodded, turned and left the ward.

Susan didn't want to think any more about any of it and tried to put all thoughts out of her mind, she would decide when she was rested, she would think better then.

Kitts left the hospital confused and worried about what would happen. He walked the streets not knowing where he was going and how he would deal with the situation his jealousy and temper had got him into.

He initially decided that it would be best if he left her, and started a new life, but then he thought 'what if she goes to the Police I'll lose my job.' He decided that he must think carefully; he had two days before work again to come to his senses and do what was right for him. She had become part of his life, but he decided his survival was more important.

Chapter 11

Kitts had walked all night after he had left the hospital; he wasn't sure what drove him and how he managed to get there and find the house, but early the next morning he banged on the wooden door desperate to talk to Mary. She was a person he knew he could trust and someone he could talk to try and explain his problem.

Answering the door nobody was more surprised than Mary Cooper to see Kitts standing there. He looked so tired and dishevelled. It took her a few seconds at first to come to her senses and realise who was actually standing there.

"Bless my soul - look at you - this is a surprise; you just left us without saying anything, what brings you back here? I thought we'd seen the last of you the way you left."

Kitts stared into her face; he couldn't speak immediately and just shook his head from side to side. Mary caught hold of his arm and pulled him gently towards the kitchen.

"You're in trouble I can tell; sit down I'll get you some hot milk and fresh bread, when you've eaten you can tell me all about it." The warmth of the drink and hot bread mixed with the old familiar smell and surroundings of Mary's kitchen calmed him. He could see Mary looking at him as he ate, and noticed she had a concerned look on her face.

When he had finished Kitts stood up, looked towards Mary and quickly blurted out "I'm sorry to be back here to bother you - I left without telling you; I know it wasn't right. I just wanted to try and better myself. It was wrong of me, I should have been honest and said from the start when I first came here that I was only working to save money so I could go to Plymouth. Since then I've got a job and met a woman, but I've got myself in bother with jealousy over her. I know I let you and Horace down but thought you would listen and help me; Mary I don't know what to do."

"Now calm down" Mary said – "you've talked an awful lot which, at the moment, don't make a lot of sense to me." Kitts smiled a bit as he remembered, she had a way of making everything seem alright, and he thought about her long talks with him trying to encourage him to converse more. He could certainly do that now and look where it had got him. Suddenly, coming back to reality, he asked "Where's Horace - is he working?"

Mary said "He's gone early to a neighbouring farm to help out with some work; we shares some help now, with you not around. I'm surprised you didn't see him."

Kitts nodded towards her, being careful not to say that he had seen a couple of people on the road but had climbed into fields before they saw him. He hadn't wanted to speak; just to remain deep in his own thoughts. He had probably done this as Horace passed him; he did remember a horse and cart going by.

Mary said "Look, I want you to sit down and talk straight to me but, before you do, it's my turn to put some things straight. I was upset when you left; you didn't say anything and just went. I felt it was my fault for being such a silly old woman and kissing you that night. It's been on my mind for a long time now. You are here though now and I can try and explain."

Kitts smiled at her and said "Oh no Mary that's not right, I always intended to leave once I had money and was able to move to Plymouth for work. Like I said I should have told you, but you were kind and I couldn't face up to telling you. I wasn't angry about what happened; just unprepared cos I didn't know how to behave. I'm ashamed to say that it was the first time anything like that had happened to me."

Mary looked a bit hurt then and said "My word you have changed since you left. I could hardly get a word out of you before. Anyway, let's have a proper talk about you and what's happened to make you like this and come back to see me."

Mary listened intently and didn't interrupt as Kitts told her about his job, his meeting with Susan, and his jealousy which had led to him becoming violent and hurting Susan. She could see that he was upset, but still let him talk on.

He had made up his mind on his journey to the farm that he was going to be truthful and tell Mary everything. He had thought also that, if he didn't go back to Plymouth, he could perhaps find farm work again, maybe back with the Cooper's; then nobody would know where he was.

Mary did not immediately reply when he had finished his tale. She just sat staring upwards at the ceiling thinking about what he had said, and wondered how she should help him. She had been taken aback by Kitt's talk about his violence. He had always seemed such a quiet person when he worked with them. Kitts found the silence and her not replying difficult; He sat fidgeting and staring at Mary hoping she would say something soon.

He was relieved when she finally spoke "I'm surprised about your violence Henry; you never ever showed that side of you when you were here. I can only think that something must have happened to you that you had not experienced before and this is what caused it. I think, as you said, it must be the jealousy of thinking she is with other men."

Kitts nodded, and wistfully Mary asked "Were you smitten with her the girl?"

Kitts could only say "yes", and tell the truth that he couldn't take his eyes off Susan when he first saw her. " I was shy" he said, "but she coaxed me; somehow as strange as it may seem, I wanted to settle down with her right away. She took an interest in me and that had never happened before; it was all so new and fast."

Mary said "But you knew she was a prostitute; did you trust her?"

"We was alright to begin with when we were together" Kitts said "but I drank, and she was out in the day; I didn't know what she was doin and thought she was with other men - she told me she wasn't and that's what started it all. Susan got very angry with me and my drinking."

Mary said "Did you hurt her badly?"

Kitts hung his head down. He knew he had to tell the truth, and said "Yes, I think I did. She's in hospital and I'm afraid she will report me and that will be my job gone - look if I don't go back will you give me work again?'

Mary shook her head; she looked at Kitts sadly, knowing that she had to convince him to do the right thing. She had to tell him now and said "No Henry, it won't be possible -you must go back and face up to what you've done. No good will be done by you running away from all this because, for certain, it will catch up with you one day. It sounds to me that you are more than just fond of her. Because of her life you can't go hurting her; you have to try and sort things out with her. It seems to me, and I'm sure you know this; you have got to stop being jealous and your heavy drinking. Besides Horace wouldn't let you stay; you must be away before he returns at nightfall, he must never know you have been here."

Kitts stared at her, realising that she was right, but was so fearful about what would happen to him. "Do I go and talk to her and see if she will have me back if I mend me ways; I have my faults, but she aint perfect either."

Mary said "Nobody is but, if you want her, you have to learn to accept each other and work at your faults. I got to say that I'm ashamed of you for your violence, it was something I never saw in you."

Kitts found himself just staring hard at the floor, taken aback by what she had said and struggled to find the right words to answer her. "I'm sorry; she were my first real time of being in the company of a woman and talking and, when I met her, the feeling I had about other men and the jealousy just drove me so that I couldn't stop; it takes me over. I didn't know it would happen, she was my first."

Mary turned away and said "You must not let it, or it'll be your downfall Henry and will wreck your life; I'll get you some food, and some for your journey, then you must be off. It's down to you now to sort it out and face up to what you did."

They ate in silence. Kitts rose and said "I have let you down I know, I'll be on me way now - thanks for listening, and I won't be back again to bother you. I aren't good with words, but am better at it now, and will always thank you for helping me"

Mary looked at his face and nodded; in a way she felt sorry for him -his background had not prepared him for the life he wanted, and she wondered if he would be able to settle and deal with his problems. Something worried her about him though which she had not previously seen, there was a change in him, she couldn't think what it was but she quickly dismissed it from her mind and hoped he could curb this violent streak within him and that it would not be his downfall.

"You take care Henry, remember what I said, don't let me or yourself down and you are right please don't come back again, it's too difficult for me."

Kitts nodded, turned, and walked across the courtyard without looking back; if he had he would have seen the tears running down Mary's cheeks.

He walked for the rest of the day, stopping only occasionally to eat or drink. He was taken back by Mary's words to him and thought a lot about what she had said. Her words had made him think and he felt bad for letting her down, but what she had said was right and it was down to him to get over his jealousy and stop drinking. He knew his faults, but if Susan would take him back and he kept his job things could be alright. He was thankful to arrive back at his old lodgings, and managed to rent a room for the night. He sat in the bar reflecting on the past events, got himself some ale and food and was enjoying it - he was now feeling famished from his walk back into Plymouth. His thoughts about what he should do were interrupted for him by a woman's voice suddenly behind him at his table. "I've been looking for you me handsome man, you're difficult to find." The sound of her voice made him jump and he nearly choked on his food as he turned to see Susan's sister Nancy, standing with her hands on her hips, but smiling. He thought that at least she didn't appear angry, or wanting to accuse him of hurting Susan. She was one of the last people he wanted to see though at that moment, as he didn't know what if anything Susan had told her.

Chapter 12

Kitts stood and faced Nancy, keeping a distance between them as he well remembered her comments to him in the Napoleon Inn telling him what she would do if he was violent towards Susan; thankfully he saw that she was still grinning and didn't appear to be angry with him at all.

She said "Let's go outside - I want to talk to you about Susan, away from the ears."

Kitts nodded, but was still concerned, and did not know what to make of this situation; was she just getting him away and outside for some other reason. He followed her, but felt ready to fend off any blows she may suddenly offer, looking around to make sure there were no others around that she had brought with her to deal with him.

She stopped a few feet from the door, turned her face towards Kitts, and said "I 'ave seen Susan in hospital, she says you came to her, but she was drowsy and didn't talk much to you about what happened."

Kitts quickly interrupted and said "What did she say, did she tell you what happened?"

Nancy said "She told me about being beaten by a man, after she told him she didn't do business anymore and that you found her and carried her to the hospital. She's worried that you might think she was back to her old ways, but she swears she did nothing." This took Kitts completely by surprise, and he hoped it didn't show in his face as he frantically tried to think of a reply. "She told you that's what happened; she was beaten by a man?"

Nancy said "Yes why - you sound surprised, is there something amiss in what she said. Is it the truth, or is she making it up for some reason?"

Kitts quickly recovered his thoughts and said "No, no, I didn't know what happened - the hospital didn't know - and I only spoke to Susan for a short while. She didn't tell me nothing, so this is all new to me."

Nancy said "She don't know who he was - or that's what she says - lucky it wasn't you that did it eh, or we wouldn't be having this talk. You'd better get there tomorrow to see her; she asked me to find you and tell you that."

Kitts gulped, trying not to look sheepish, and said "Yes I will, we need to speak and I need to find out exactly what 'appened to her, and help her out."

Nancy smiled at him again and said "Yeh you do that and, whilst she's in there, I got you all to myself haven't I - my old man's away so we are both on our own. Who knows?"

Kitts took a step backwards; this worried him and surprised him with her speaking like that.

Nancy laughed and started to walk away and, as she left, she looked over her shoulder smiling and said "Make sure you do -

perhaps you can find who did it, and show them they was wrong to touch her; I'll look out for you."

Kitts was stunned by the conversation that had just taken place and stood there trying to work out what was happening. He went and sat on the step of a nearby shop, and put his head in his hands trying to work out in his own mind exactly what was happening. He didn't trust Nancy, or was it a case that he didn't know her. Her comments were completely different to what he expected and he was searching her words for some catch, or was there one? Perhaps it was just him being suspicious. Could be Susan had thought about it and wanted him back to settle down again. She had also made suggestions to him which had also caught him off his guard. Nancy obviously fancied her chances with him whilst Susan was out of the way. He thought about this - she was an attractive woman, but it would only lead him into more bother, and he already had enough. This must be put into the back of his mind. The trouble was he had no experience of how women's' minds worked. The sight of a Policeman though walking up the road brought him back to reality and the best thing he could do for now would be head for his own room for the night. It was Sunday the next day and he remembered what Mary had said. Yes, he must be strong and must face up to everything. She was right he thought, that's the only way I'm going to find out what's happening.

This thought did nothing to allay his fears that something was wrong with the story and he spent a restless night imagining all sorts of situations.

Kitts got out of bed in the morning, washed his face with cold water and convinced himself that this was a trap to catch him Oh yes – it had to be a trap - and the police would be waiting for him at the hospital. Despite the fact he also knew that Susan could tell the Police where he probably stayed, it did nothing to remove the thought from his mind. He stayed in his room during the morning pacing up and down and thinking about things to say depending on what happened. He left by the back door of the Inn keeping to the side streets as much as he could as he made his way to the hospital. It was made more difficult by the fact that he only knew roughly where it was, and he did ask directions once. He made sure he was not followed, looking over his shoulder every few yards and checking carefully around corners before proceeding into the roads. As he reached the outskirts of the hospital he stopped and sat on a wall watching the entrance and checking who came and went. He wanted to be sure everything was as Nancy had said. He had only been there a few minutes when, sure enough, a Policeman walked out of the door of the hospital – stopped - looked up and down the road and then started to walk in his direction. He quickly scurried off the way he had come, turning down the first road on his left. Whilst out of sight of the Policeman Kitts ran, looking over his shoulder every so often to see if he was being pursued. He was out of breath and, bending over, had to stop to catch his wind, He looked up and, to his dismay, saw that the road he had been running down in front of him was a dead-end. Oh no, he thought – looking around. He looked could see that the only way out was to retrace his steps back towards the hospital. It took him a few minutes to recover. He walked slowly back, watching as he approached the junction for any signs that the policeman had seen him. He stopped on the corner, carefully looking towards the hospital and then down the road, being very relieved to see the policeman talking to a man well away from the junction. He quickly walked in the other direction and made his way into the hospital, but was ready to change direction if he needed to.

Having reached the door of Susan's ward he stopped, thought about what he was going to say, but decided he would first see what Susan said. Fortunately, there was a gap in the door and he could look through. To his relief Kitts saw that Susan was alone and sat up in bed. He made his way tentatively towards her bed. She saw him approaching and said "Where've yer been -you should have been here earlier the police have just gone. They were looking for you."

Kitts stared, felt the anger boiling up inside him and said "Your bloody sister said you told her you were attacked by a punter, and now you got the police looking for me. I knew I couldn't trust her, she lied"

Susan looked straight at him and angrily said "What a bloody greeting after what you done to me; I did tell her that, and the police were told by her the same story, and that's what they was 'ere for. They want to see you about it, to ask where you found me, they don't think you done it, I didn't drop you in it but, my god, you deserves it you bastard. All you thinks about is saving your own bloody neck"

Kitts was taken back and lost for words when he realised that she had covered for him and his running up and down side streets to avoid the police had all been because of his own fear and mistrust. He hung his head, searching rapidly for the right answer to appease Susan and said "I was wrong - I didn't understand why you made up the story when I was to blame for what 'appened to you. Why 'ave you done that. I don't deserve it I got all mixed up in me head about what was 'appening."

Susan said "No, you'm right, I might change me mind and then you'd be running scared. I thought you might be pleased after your harm to me but it seems you were only thinking about your own neck again you bastard."

Kitts knelt down beside her bed so that his face was level with hers and asked her "Did you want us to be together again, is that why you done it?"

Susan didn't reply immediately; she looked away from him and said in a quiet voice "I was prepared to forgive you this time, but this is the last time I would add. I wants off the street and you and me was a way out. Then you hits me and puts me 'ere, what am I supposed to do or think."

Kitts knew he had to come up with the right answer if he was to keep her and thought quickly and said "Yes, I wanted that, you off the street, I was worried about losing me job over it then we wouldn't have any money to live; that's what I was thinking about, us. I didn't want you on the street because of no money, if you forgive me, we can try again."

Kitts knew he had thought up this answer, in line with what she had just said, and he hoped that she would be convinced about his reply. He desperately Wanted Susan to believe him. He looked pleadingly at her and she half smiled saying "You are a bastard Enry but, if that's really what you was thinking, we could try again - but you knows there will be no more violence, nobody has ever wanted me other than for me body. I've ad enough of that life, look at me I'm wrecked. Kitt smiled and leaned over, gently kissing her cheek and feeling satisfied that she had accepted his reasons - even though he knew that his main concern was not getting arrested. She was right about that and he hoped he didn't show it. He knew things wouldn't be easy and it wasn't a perfect life for him, but keeping his job and having a woman to satisfy and feed him would keep him happy.

Kitts left the ward feeling reasonably satisfied that everything had more or less gone his way. He could tolerate the life as long as she didn't go back to her old ways. This was the one thing that caused him to lose his temper and he knew it had been the cause of all their previous problems and his violence. They could only try and hope.

Chapter 13

Whilst Susan was hospitalised Henry Kitts spent his time working but, during the rest of his time, he was still drinking, he felt there was nothing else to do. This to him had become the norm and, although he woke up each day feeling terrible - with an aching head and had great difficulty rising for work - by the late afternoon he had recovered. This was always a mystery to him and he couldn't work out how, after feeling so bad, by the end of work he always felt ready to drink again, having forgotten the headaches and tiredness it caused. He managed to fit in the occasional visit to Susan telling her he was carrying out extra work that had to be finished on time, and was too tired to visit every day. He felt he had to do this in order for her to stay with him and also it would cover up his heavy drinking. He knew he was fond of her and got jealous but also, he knew the drink was once again ruling his life and this would have to stop when she left hospital. Susan was not totally convinced of his reasons for not visiting. She had smelt drink on him several times early in the evening, but hadn't said anything to him as she lived in the hope that, when she was discharged, they would sort everything out; maybe he was only drinking because she wasn't there with him. At least he wasn't with another women Susan thought but she didn't want to think about this as well. That would just play on her mind to during the long days spent lying on her bed. All of this had of course caused her to wonder several times if she was making the right decision. They had talked about it so many times before though and had both agreed that the drinking, violence, and her work on the streets were over. She just lived in the hope that this is what would happen, and there would be some normality for once in her life. She would lie on her hospital bed and yearn for this settled life now; Susan had endured enough violence and abuse and this was her one chance to make something of her life if only Kitts could settle down and keep his side of the bargain. She wanted to go home but they had insisted she stayed longer to allow her to rest and return herself to a more settled state of normality.

Kitts had also made a point of presenting himself at the Police Station now that he knew he was safe from any blame or suspicion. It had taken him a while to do this and he had felt nervous during the time he was there - wishing that the officer would hurry and not ask so many questions.

He had told the officer how he had found Susan in the street, near to their room, but he didn't know any more than what she had said. He felt relieved now this had been done and he would be able to resume his normal life without the fear of looking over his shoulder all the time thinking he may be arrested. He did think the officer had looked at him in a strange quizzical way when he told the story, but it was clear nothing else was known and Susan had backed up his story. They had nothing else to think he was involved.

He moved back to Susan's room and he now felt safe from the law; he didn't have to be careful either where he went or stayed. Yes, he was free from the worry. Most nights he was drunk and unsteady on his feet, but he knew from his most recent visit to Susan that she was being discharged very soon. He would have to be careful about his drinking and tidy the room - which he hadn't bothered to do since arriving. He worked and drank and, as far as he was concerned, there was no time for cleaning rooms, Susan would do that. He didn't want Susan to know the life he had been living though so must keep his eye on when she would be let out. Tonight, though was no different for him; he hadn't visited Susan and had spent all evening drinking in the Napoleon.

He stumbled against the door as he entered their room, gazing through bleary eyes into the semi darkened room only partly lit by the glow of a light somewhere outside. He threw his clothes in a heap on the floor and climbed onto the bed just as a voice suddenly said "So this is what you do whilst my sister is in hospital, come here." Kitts leapt back in shock and surprise, at the same time trying to stand up on unsteady legs; his heart was pounding as Nancy grabbed his arms and he was pulled onto the bed.

She said "You're mine tonight - just for the one night. I've fancied you since Susan took me to the Napoleon. She's away, and it's a long time since my man was home."

Kitts was drunk and couldn't think of a reply or even want to. He was too far gone to protest, even though he thought he should, she was undressed and he willingly climbed in beside Nancy. He thought 'What the hell she wants me.'

Next morning, he woke with a thumping head and little memory of what happened, surprised to see Nancy there beside him. He slowly began to remember her being in his bed when he came home - starting to panic about the situation – saying "What have we done? Don't tell Susan, she'll never understand; I'll lose the roof over me head."

Nancy got out of bed, started dressing and, turning towards him with a scornful look, said "Don't worry - there's nothing to tell; she's welcome to you, the drink don't do you any favours. I shan't say anything and you won't have anything to boast about trust me."

Kitts didn't bother to reply and watched as Nancy finished dressing in silence, looking away when she glared at him before leaving the room.

Kitts sat on the bed; his head was pounding as he held it in his hands. Her remarks, although directed at his lack of passion, made him feel somewhat relieved about the situation. He was sure she wouldn't say anything; it was her sister and she wouldn't want to explain to her.

This made him feel somewhat easier. He hurriedly got dressed, tidied the room this time to make sure there were no traces of

Nancy, and left for work. As he walked he thought he must go to the hospital after work and find out exactly when Susan was coming home. Also, he would know then what time he had left to enjoy his life of drink.

Kitts walked into the hospital after work and the antiseptic smell, that seemed to be a permanent feature of the place, did nothing to relieve his pounding head, which had (for some reason today) failed to clear as the day went on. He put it down to having a headache through trying to sort out all the problems - with the added one of the previous night. Pulling himself up straight he walked into the ward and was surprised to see Susan dressed and sat on the bed with her belongings looking towards the door. Putting on a smile, he tried to look pleased as he walked towards her bed, but was thinking that his drinking was now over; oh yes, it had to be, and Susan was ready to leave.

"I knew you'd come - that's why I got ready - I can go.'" Susan said.

Kitts reached out, caught hold her arm as she stood, picked up her belongings saying "Come on then - let's get you out of 'ere - the smell in this place don't do me any good at all." He was angry inside though about not being able to go drinking tonight; he had thought he would have had more warning of Susan's discharge and really needed more time to adjust to it. He must not show his anger though he thought; just keep quiet.

Susan clutched his arm as they walked, and complained he was walking too fast; there was little conversation between them, but she was glad to be out of hospital. Her thoughts were directed on the future which she hoped would turn out as she wanted. They reached their room and Kitts placed Susan's belongings on the bed. She said "Has Nancy been in and done things for you - she said she'd look after you?"

This remark made Kitts look at her before quickly saying "yes." Glancing around the room he thought she can't know anything about last night, that's not possible. She must have seen something – had she seen something? Anyway, the conversation wasn't pursued thank goodness, and he decided it was just him being jumpy.

Kitts - desperate for a drink – saw his chance saying "Now that you're home shall we go to the Napoleon to celebrate?"

Susan readily agreed and said "Yeh - alright you can spend some of that extra money you've been earning on - I could do with a drink, its days since I had some."

Kitts looked at her but didn't reply, happy that he at least could drink with her.

The night ended in a drunken stupor for both of them and it took only a few more weeks for their lives to return to the way it had been, with continual drinking and shortage of money dominating their lives, causing the same frictions, and leading to more arguments.

Chapter 14

The weeks following her discharge from hospital had merged and, during the morning of Thursday 15th July, Susan Foster scrubbed their room. She moved the brush vigorously across the floor, finding this helped release the anger and tension that had built up inside her. She was without food and penniless again. Since she had left hospital they still argued about the same things, but at least he had not been violent again towards her though, at times, it had been close. She had managed to avoid the violence by shouting and warning him that she would leave if it started again. She knew it had come close on several occasions but her shouts lately seemed to bring him to his senses and he would back off.

Kitts returned home for his mid-day meal as usual but there was only bread for him on the table Susan ignored him and sat facing away from him, busying herself by pretending to sew and repair a skirt. The lack of a proper meal led to another round of verbal abuse between the two of them. Kitts stormed out of the room - having heard enough - slamming the door as he left and Susan shouting after him "Get some bloody money, and then you will have some proper food on the table." She didn't believe his talk of getting money later that day; she'd heard it all before. Susan now decided she must get out of the cramped room and perhaps somehow get some money herself; she wasn't sure how, she thought about one way - but dismissed it for the time being. That way would have to wait, it was too soon. The day had got off to a bad start and she wished again that things were different.

Susan leaned out the front of the house, eyeing the lane carefully in both directions before leaving the door and walked briskly towards the High Street - ignoring the smells which were more than familiar to her.

She was propelled by the anger that had built up inside her. She needed a drink to calm her, but didn't have any money and decided to seek out her sister who may well have a few coins she could borrow for a drink, and then get food for some supper. The street, as normal, was busy with a mix of people of all ages and backgrounds. She didn't particularly want to meet or speak to anyone, and kept her head down not looking at any faces. Susan crossed the cobbled street, avoiding the horse dung, glancing towards the window of the local outfitters as she had done many times before. If she thought about it she probably did it most times as she passed the shop. She stopped and, as she did so, she momentarily stared down at her soiled faded skirt and then looked at the dress in the window. She always wished she could dress like some of the women she had seen in all their lovely finery. The skirt she was wearing she had on most days - having just mended it. Susan only possessed one other dress which was only slightly better. She yearned to leave her poor existence behind. To own dresses like those in the window was her wish but she knew, only too well, that was a very distant possibility at this time. She also remembered that she was banned from most of the shops for stealing and some would only let her enter if she showed she had money. She sighed, put the thoughts out of her head and walked towards the Naval Reserve Inn, the regular haunt of her sister, and entered the crowded bar. It was busy and difficult to see clearly through the smoke, all mixed up with the smell of drink.

Bill the landlord spotted her entering, laughed and shouted "Hello Sue, what brings you here you old tart, there's plenty for you to choose from today."

She nodded, didn't look at him, half raised her hand in a greeting, but didn't feel like replying pushing her way through the drinkers searching for her sister.'

His remark made her angry; people would not accept her change. It seemed to her that, if women no longer sold themselves, they did not welcome them back easily and they were always branded. Susan knew she was poor but felt she still had some pride. She wanted people to accept this, and the fact she had given up working the street. Her prostitution had been the result of necessity and she was far from proud of the fact, and how she had turned out.

She forced her way around the bar, looking around and satisfying herself her sister was not there. She made her way through the crowd towards the door, ignoring the coarse remarks and trying to fend off the hands she could feel touching and reaching out for her.

Once back in High Street Susan crossed the road and walked up the slope, waving to Liz Elliot who ran the second-hand clothes shop where she bargained for most of her clothes. That was rare though these days as money was scarce. She liked Liz, who had been kind to her in the past and had given her cast off items to wear; she was someone she felt could be trusted, but she was probably only one of a few.

The Napoleon Inn was her next call; she made her way towards the bar, accepted a drink, and then sat at the rear of the smoke-filled room. Her eyes were stinging from the smoke. She could see her sister was not there and by now did not feel inclined to look further. She'd had enough. Money would have to come another way.

She held her glass of ale with both hands, occasionally bringing it to her lips but only sipping it. She still felt the anger inside and was staring, thinking as she looked towards the assortment of customers who congregated near the corner of the bar. She recognized and knew most, either intimately from her past or as people who worked or regularly frequented the area. Looking at them added to her anger, as she knew they thought nothing of her. She knew they all had used her in the past, but they as well would not accept that she was trying to make a new life. Whenever they saw her they would tug at her clothing and make suggestive remarks as she passed them by.

She had been grateful to Adam the bar boy who had joked with her and slipped her the glass of ale on seeing her enter the bar. Susan had known his mother Maisie who had worked the streets with her. Maisie, who was older, had looked after her when her mother died and when she first plied her trade. Maisie had struck lucky one day, marrying a wealthy punter who owned property in the area who had fallen for her. Susan saw very little of Maisie now but, when she did, Maisie always offered her food or help in other ways.

She had accepted the drink from Adam but she knew, as thoughts tore through her mind, that her anger had not brought her to the Napoleon just to drink - she needed money. Kitts was to blame for all this she thought; he drinks away his money and I am left with nothing. Anger rose in her as she thought 'I kept my side of the bargain. He ill-treats me, and I put up with it.'

Her thoughts of Kitts now were far from endearing.

Taking a further sip from her ale, Susan's eyes drifted to the side of the bar towards a group of seamen that were noisily celebrating their time ashore. She was careful not to make eye contact with them, as she didn't want to have to fend off their advances.

She thought how these men in the past would have been her company. She would have enjoyed it and the eventual opportunity to relieve them of their hard-earned money.

She also thought about the violence that she had sometimes met and the risks of disease. A guilty feeling came over her at all her mixed thoughts; she remembered the promise she had made to Kitts, although she also thought of the violence he had used. She was surprised at the feelings of guilt as she had never felt these in the past. The promises he had made about looking after her and providing for her keep had diminished over the months they had been together - why should she worry?

His increasing drinking and violence towards her had made her feel he was not the same man she had met. She blamed it on the company he kept from work; many of them were hard drinkers. Glancing up Susan saw that the crowd of seamen were leaving, noticing the glass of rum that had been left by one of them on the side. She quickly rose and picked up the glass, returning to her table where she poured it into her ale. She then looked towards the bar, checking to see if Jim who owned the Napoleon had seen her, and was happy to see he was not in his usual place behind the bar. He tolerated her but had previously warned her, following a disturbance involving some fishermen refusing to pay for services she had provided.

She partly felt relief at seeing the seamen leave which, mixed with her feeling of guilt, prevented her making an approach to them - though she thought that bastard Henry deserved it. Susan sipped her drink, almost choking on the first mouthful of the strong mixture. Her mind drifted to the time when she had met Kitts and how well they had got on when they first lived together - although she did remember being worried about his temper and jealousy.

She sipped away on the mixture, deep in thoughts, and was suddenly brought back to her senses by a glass of ale being placed on her table. Looking up, she smiled as she recognised Maisie stood in front of her and said "Ello what you doin ere, I avn't seen you for a long while, I was only thinking about you just now?"

Maisie laughed and said "Sorry I woke you Foss; you looked like you was dreaming. I was in the area collecting some rent money and came to see me boy as well; he said you was here and I thought I would come and see you."

Susan said "That's good - it's nice to ave someone I can talk to."

Maisie said "Tell me about your man, you look worn out - I hope you're not spending too much time on your back, or against a wall you old devil."

Susan said "No, I packed up all that, but things aint good, he drinks - has no money and ill-treats me; we are rowing all the time.'

Maisie could see tears beginning to well up in Susan's eyes, and moved from her seat to be beside her, putting her arm around her shoulder and holding her close.

She said "Tell me about it, I'll get us another drink."

The two sat drinking and Susan told her about Kitts and how he had started drinking heavily, which had led to rows and him knocking her around and her finishing up in hospital.

Maisie listened quietly to her story and said "Don't let the bastard get the better of you, kick him out."

Susan didn't reply right away, looking towards the floor; she knew she was right, but she also knew it wouldn't be easy. He was strong, had been violent towards her but also, if he left, she would once again drift back into her old ways. She also thought that regardless of what he thought she had not gone back to her old ways Despite all that happened she still had a certain fondness for Kitts but 'God knows why' she thought.

Susan looked up at Maisie and said "Yeh I know, I'm just bloody worried about what will happen to me, my life is just getting worse; I thought we was going to make something better the two of us and settle down properly."

Maisie bought another drink saying Look, I'm no angel, I just struck lucky. Who knows, you may get lucky to; but, look I got to be off or he'll start thinking I'm back to my old ways. We can't have that - there's too much to lose."

Maisie gave her a hug, smiled, and winked as she left. Susan remained in her seat finishing her ale, watching Masie move through the drinkers, sighing to herself and thinking about what she said and what could happen. If only Kitts didn't drink, get jealous and hurt her, it would be just like when they first got together. They was good times she thought. Maisie was a good friend but she hadn't really helped her, but of course she was a friend and someone who would support her in her own way. Susan brought herself back to reality and had to admit she was feeling light headed with all the drink and, at that moment, felt quite happy. She decided to sit there and enjoy the moment.

Chapter 15

Kitts had left the room angry about the lack of food and walked back to work, eating pieces of bread he had snatched from the table - silently cursing Susan to himself as he strode along, not caring who he bumped into; people could see him walking aggressively in their direction, and moved well out of his way before he had the opportunity to push them aside.

During the afternoon, whilst laying ballast for the tracks, he thought about their rows and life together - they were two sided as far as he could work out. He was not happy with the way Susan was behaving and thought she may well have gone back to her old ways - drinking and men; the thought of this made him angry and jealous. From her side, as far as he could make out, she was always accusing him of having no money and drinking. The drinking was true, he knew that; he did drink more but, as far as he was concerned, this was his way of dealing with his problems - it made him feel better and stopped his thoughts about what she might be up to. Kitts thought long and hard about leaving Susan but, in his own way, he was still fond of her; when things were good she provided all, he could want as a man. If only she would change her ways, and stop making him jealous. He did not at that moment want to consider what he was doing, and what she thought. He gradually calmed, down reflecting on his thoughts, and decided that he would approach his employer Mr Relph to ask for a sub until pay day and try to resolve his lack of money he could give her; this might make her happier and it would let her know that he was trying to sort out their differences. He felt relieved after he saw his employer who, after some bargaining, allowed him two shillings advance from his pay. This felt good in his pocket and he knew he must resist the urge to spend it on drink on his way home.

Kitts finished work for the day and walked back towards Lower Lane, jangling the coins in his trouser pocket as he walked, now feeling that he would give her some money and try with her. He thought about what he would say and hoped that this would at least keep her off his back. He would do his best not to drink so much - have more money - and felt that, if things returned to how they were between them, he wouldn't need to drink and would be happier with his life and with her. So much had happened to him in the way of changes since he left home; there had been the advances of Mary but he had to admit, the more he thought about it, it was certainly more than fondness for Susan. He had become obsessed with her but his uncontrollable jealousy was the cause of his behaviour towards her.

He reached their house, pushed open the front door and went to their room, but there was no sign of Susan; there was no fire lit for cooking and he couldn't see any sign of food. He went and banged on her sister's door but there was no reply. His plans to placate matters and give her some money suddenly changed. He felt anger building up inside him – turned, slammed the door, and walked briskly towards the High Street. Had she walked out and left him, or had she gone back to her old ways to get money? His mind was racing with all these thoughts as he made his way into the Naval Reserve. The bar was crowded as he pushed his way around, but there was no sign of Susan. He was certainly not going to ask if anyone had seen her - he would find her himself, and find out what she had been up to.

Kitts hurried up High street and made his way into the bar of the Napoleon - immediately seeing Susan sitting at the back of the bar sipping ale. Susan saw him through a kind of haze as he made his way to her table. He stood in front of her and reached out to grab her arm. She pushed his arm away, standing up and facing him across the table and staring into his angry face. Moving his face close to hers and speaking through clenched teeth he said "I want you to come home with me."

'Susan said "I'll come home when I'm ready, and don't lay a hand on me. I told you before what I would do." She smiled at him as she said it, feeling full of confidence with the drink inside her.

Kitts pushed her shoulder, causing her to fall back into the chair. He turned and walked out of the Napoleon; as he left not looking back.

Susan picked up her ale, draining the last remains, standing and feeling slightly unsteady on her feet; she thought 'I'm ready now, I had better go home, but I suppose it will be another row and more threats of violence. She made her way to the door, feeling the warm summer air hit her face as she made her way into High street, and finding it difficult at times to walk in a straight line. She smiled to herself again, feeling light headed.

Susan made her way into their room, nearly losing her balance as she pushed open the door.

As she came in Kitts was stood in the centre of the room facing her and shouted "Why were you not at home to get my supper?

You had no business to be in that Inn drinking, you were looking for men."

Susan said "I wasn't, I was looking for me sister for money; I will get your supper now I suppose."

Kitts stepped quickly towards her and said "I'll teach you" and he pushed her on the chest causing her to lose her balance. She fell back against the bedpost hitting her head - crying out "You bastard, there's no need to push me."

Susan started to scream for help, shouting "I told you I would leave you if you hit me again." Kitts kicked the table, causing china to smash on the floor and said "You'll learn to be here when I come home." She started to stand up from beside the bed; he came towards her, and pushing her with both hands, causing her to fall on the floor backwards, hitting her head against some of the broken china.

Susan screamed out as her head hit the floor. She felt dazed, partly through the drink and partly because of the blow to her head. She put her hand to the back of her head and saw that it was covered in blood. She decided not to shout or cry out any more as this would just antagonise him even further. She held the back of her head, sobbing quietly as she started warily to stand up - watching Kitts, and expecting a further blow. The door suddenly flew open and her sister ran into the room shouting "I heard the screams, what's going on?" She came towards Susan and, smelling the drink on her, shouted "Susan you ought not to drink" and turned towards Kitts who was leaning over Susan. Nancy pushed him aside and said "You ought not to strike her; I have told you both about this before, if you can't live comfortably you two had better part."

She helped Susan to her feet and led her out of the room past Kitts and, staring straight at him, said "You've cut her, she has blood on the back of her head, it is bleeding." They went through the front door and onto the street.

The noise of the disturbance had attracted people into the street and others looked out of their windows wanting to know what was happening.

Kitts followed them out to the street; Susan and her sister picked up some dry horse dung from the street and started throwing it at Kitts who was trying to come towards them to hit out at Susan. They screamed at him to stop and the shouts were heard by PC Bennett, who was in the area and had just walked from High Street into Lower Lane. Susan and her sister both spotted him coming towards them and her sister shouted out "I'd give him in charge."

PC Bennett walked towards Susan asking "What's all the shouting about -you are all disturbing the peace. "Susan put her hand up to the back of her head and pointed at Kitts. She said "See ow I'm bleeding I give him in charge - my ead is bleeding - I give him in charge."

Kitts heard this, panicked and turned, pushing his way past people stood watching the disturbance and, nearly knocking a man over, ran back into the house climbing the stairs two at a time. He wasn't sure where he was going but was being propelled by the panic of hearing Susan talk to the Policeman. He knew he must try and hide. He ran up to the top of the house and tried to open the garret door, but it was stuck fast and he could only open it slightly. There was no way he could hide in the garret; he started sweating and panicking trying to think of what to do next to avoid the Police. Pc Bennett ran into the house, stopped, and stood in the hallway trying to work out where Kitts had gone, and listening for sounds. Mary Williams, a widow who lived on the top floor and who had been watching the disturbance on the street from her window, came out onto the landing hearing Kitts on the next floor pulling at the garret door. She shouted down the stairs "He's up here on the next floor trying to get in the garret." She pushed her door almost closed, wedging her foot against it and peering through the crack so she could see what was happening. She didn't want to get involved, but wanted to see everything.

PC Bennett ran up the three flights of stairs, saw Kitts by the garret door and, as he approached him, shouted out "Stay there, you've caused enough trouble." Kitts came towards him to try and push past - PC Bennett, trying to grab hold of him, caught his clothing but the movement of Kitts going forward caused the pair of them to fall down the stairs onto the landing outside Mary Williams's door - with Kitts landing on top of the Policeman. On seeing this Mary Williams quickly closed her door tight, and ran to her window, opened it, and shouted to the crowd below "For God's sake come up or else there will be a murder committed."

Bennett struggled, trying to push Kitts off him as his knee was on his chest and his own head was turned and jammed in the corner against the wall. He felt weak and breathless and unable to push Kitts very hard. He wondered why he felt like that and, despite being in the struggle, thought it must be the running up the stairs that had caused this effect.

Thomas Harvey, who was a well-built local porter living in Lower Lane, had heard the row in the street and had come outside; he'd joined the crowd, and seen what was happening. He had heard Mary Williams, who he knew had shouted from her window. Harvey ran into the house, up the stairs, grabbed Kitts by the shoulders, pulled him off without a struggle and held his arm and said "Policeman get up I'm here." PC Bennett was out of breath, but struggled to his feet, even though he felt light headed. He caught his breath and said to Kitts in a strained voice "You go quiet; I am taking you to the station." Kitts nodded towards him and let himself be led down the stairs with PC Bennett in front and Harvey behind him. On reaching the door and going onto the street Bennett held one arm and Harvey held his other arm and grabbed his collar. They started to walk through the crowd that had gathered outside and had walked a few steps when Kitts suddenly fell to the ground, which caused Bennett to be dragged down as well. Harvey thought this was all an act on his part and managed to still keep hold of Kitts arm; he said "Come on get up out of this." He pulled Kitts back onto his feet and unbuttoned his shirt collar; then he put his hand around his throat, more as a warning and to prevent him using any possible violence. PC Bennett managed to stand again but felt breathless and was still light headed. He needed a few moments to catch his breath again before saying "There will be no more of this, let him go now, we will walk him to the station." The three continued to walk a few more yards and had reached Middle Lane by St Andrews Street when Kitts fell again – but, this time he was firmly held by the arms. PC Bennett said "You had better hold him down" but Kitts said "No, I will walk quietly." Harvey looked at PC Bennett, who he could see was struggling, and said to Kitts "Well, we'll give you one more chance and, if you don't go quietly, I'll put you on quick and give you what you want." Kitts, who despite his own strength realised that Harvey was more powerful, and meant it and said "All right'." PC Bennett was struggling to focus his eyes and breathe properly as they let Kitts stand. He felt hot and dizzy and Harvey said to Kitts "Don't play anymore tricks." They started to move but PC Bennett was struggling to breathe and gasped "I'm licked, I can go no further."

Kitts knew he was in trouble, but realised that something was wrong with the Policeman, which worried him as he would be blamed for it and so he said "You go in Policeman, I'll go quietly with him" indicating Harvey.

William Smale who had been drawn to the area by the noise and crowd had been watching proceedings; he saw that PC Bennett was in difficulty, struggling to stand, and ran towards him. He held his right arm tight to support him and said "I'll take you and sit you down." PC Bennett could hardly breathe but allowed himself to be led into Barrett's shop, also assisted now on his other arm by Frank Twitchell the innkeeper of the Swan Inn - who had seen what was happening and had run to help him.

PC Bennett was sat on a chair. Twitchell said "Where's your helmet?" Bennett was gasping for air now, saying "I don't know." Twitchell could see that he was struggling to breathe and, running from the shop, returned with a glass of brandy. He put it down beside PC Bennett and unbuttoned the officer's tunic as he said "I'm choking give me air."

Twitchell turned, went forward pushing everyone away from the door, shouting for them to clear the area, as Smale picked up the glass and tried to give him the brandy. PC Bennett could not swallow it though and vomited frothing now at the mouth. Smale wiped off Bennett's mouth with his sleeve and said "Have you been kicked?"

PC Bennett gasped "No not kicked, I am dying give me air" and then slumped forward, falling off the chair to the floor. He was dead.

By this time PC Strang had just arrived and, on seeing what had happened, ran to try and get a doctor, but it was too late.

Chapter 16

Harvey continued to walk Kitts towards the Station House without him causing any more trouble. He was met by a Policeman making his way towards the disturbance, who at first looked surprised to see him holding a man by the arm and leading him along the street. He stopped them and asked what they were up to. Harvey said, 'There was a disturbance by this man with Susan Foster who shouted at PC Bennett to take him in. My names Harvey by the way, I lives near them, and knows of them, I saw a lot of what happened. There was a struggle between PC Bennett and him and the Policeman was hurt and couldn't go any further so I said I would take him to the station house'. Kitts shook his head whilst listening to this but decided not to say anything at that moment. The Policeman looked at Kitts and said, 'Right you will come back with me to sort this matter out with the Sergeant, and can you come as well Mr Harvey, we shall need you as a witness'.

The Policeman took hold of Kitts who did not put up any resistance, and said, 'What's your name?'

'It's Henry Kitts, it was all Fosters doing though, I'll tell my side of it.'

The three then made their way to the station house without any further conversation between them.

News of the incident had of course reached the Police, as several people had run in and told them of a disturbance in Lower Lane, but nobody at that time realised that Bennett had died. The Superintendent who was on duty had left to take control and establish exactly what had happened.

On arrival Kitts was taken to be seen by the sergeant. The circumstances as they knew them were explained both by Harvey and the Policeman, with Harvey relating how he had helped PC Bennett. The Sergeant scratched his head, said nothing for a few seconds before looking at Kitts and said, 'This sounds a serious matter with you fighting one of my officers.

You will be detained here as there is obviously a complaint about you assaulting this woman Foster, and we will need to speak to PC Bennett to find out what he has to say about his dealings with you'

Kitts said, 'It was all her fault, I didn't mean to hurt anyone, we fell'

The Sergeant then said, 'Take him to the locked room and stay with him till we know what's going on, and watch him carefully'.

Kitts was led to the room near the cells and sat with his head in his hands, not speaking, just looking at the floor, trying to think how all this had happened, how had it got to this stage? He hoped that the Policeman was alright to save himself any further trouble.

Harvey was asked to sit in a room beside the station house entrance.

Superintendent Frederick Wreford walked to Lower Lane and was directed by the crowd into Barrett's shop, where Frank

Twitchell, who knew the Superintendent said, 'I'm sorry sir he's dead, he couldn't go on with the Prisoner, Tom Harvey took him in though, he just fell over we tried to help him with a drink and that'.

The Superintendent was taken back to see PC Bennett on the ground with froth coming from his mouth. He was a good officer, and held in high esteem and he knew that he had only been married a few months. He knelt down beside him, placed his hand gently on his neck, he was still warm, but it was obvious he was dead.

PC Strang arrived back at the shop, approached Superintendent Wreford who was still kneeling and said,' Sir, I went back for the Police Doctor, he's being sent for'.

Wreford was upset but stood and said, 'make arrangements for PC Bennett to be taken to the station house, the doctor will examine him there'. Wreford knew he must compose himself and take full charge of the incident and cleared his throat turning towards the other officers and said,' speak to all the witnesses, obtain statements and make sure that Susan Foster is found and brought immediately to the station house'

Two of the officers fetched a stretcher and carefully lifted and placed PC Bennett on it and slowly walked back to the Station House with his body. Crowds had gathered and were keen to try and find out what had happened and see what the officers were doing. Rumour and speculation had already started, and the crowds made the officers progress difficult. On arrival the stretcher was carried through the station passing the room in which Kitts was pacing up and down; the door was open with a Policeman stood outside. On seeing Bennetts body Kitts who had no idea that he had been fatally injured shouted, 'Oh no he isn't dead tell me, I didn't kill him we fell together'

Kitts dropped to the floor sobbing with his hands on his face. The Policeman at the door went to him pulling him up onto his feet and placed him on a chair, at the same time pushing the door closed with his foot.

Bennett's body was taken into a back room and the stretcher placed across a table.

Williams the Coroners Officer had arrived followed by Sedley Wolferstan the Police Surgeon, who was seen by Superintendent Wreford and updated as to what was known about the incident.

The three men went to Bennett's body where Wolferstan certified death then physically examined in detail the head and upper body areas, but could find no signs of any violence, but noted that there was froth coming from his mouth. He said to Williams,' Contact Mr Brian the Coroner and ask him to meet me here as soon as possible, this is a serious matter, and one of possible murder'.

Thomas Cadwaller Brian was an experienced Coroner having been appointed to the Borough in 1868, having previously been the solicitor for the Post Office. He had dealt with many incidents within the Borough and was respected for his judgements and opinion by all within the local legal professions. He attended the Station House where he was briefed by Wolferstan and Wreford and following his brief examination of Bennett's body immediately ordered that a post mortem be carried out by Wolferstan and that an inquest would take place afterwards with all witnesses being examined at the Coroners Inquisition.

Superintendent Wreford immediately left the room and briefed his Sergeant to ensure that statements were being obtained from the witnesses and that they were made available for the inquest the following day. He repeated his request for Foster to be found and brought to him at the station where he would interview her with another officer.

Susan Foster had left the scene of the disturbance in a hurry making sure she was not followed, and walked out onto High

Street. It was getting out of hand as far as she was concerned and she didn't want to be involved any more so made her way to the hospital, where the wound on her head was found to be superficial and was bandaged and then discharged.

Susan walked slowly back towards her house not knowing the full extent as to what had happened, she had left before either Kitts or the Policeman had left the house. She slowly turned from the High street into Lower Lane and was immediately seen by a Policeman stood near the door to her house. He shouted, 'Foster come here', and hurried towards her grabbing her by the arm. Susan tried to wriggle free shouting, 'what are you doing, I aint done nothing Kitts caused this on me ead I've been to the hospital'

The Policeman said, 'Pc Bennetts dead and your man Kitts is at the Station House, the Superintendent wants to talk to you about what happened'

Foster looked horrified, screamed, burst into tears and between sobs said, 'it's nothing I done, Kitts was fighting with him on the stairs when I left, I was hurt by him meself, look at the back of my head'

Foster was marched by the arm to the Station House where Superintendent Wreford took her into his office accompanied by the Police officer who had brought her in.

Wreford said,' I want you to tell me what you remember about earlier today PC Bennett is dead and your man Kitts is here for his murder'.

Foster still sobbing said, 'I can't believe it but I left after we had a row I went to hospital I hit me head on the fender when he pushed me'.

Wreford said, 'when did you see the Policeman, what did you say and did you see him struggling with Kitts?'

Foster said, 'I saw him in the street and said something like he tried to murder me and yes I saw them two fighting on the stairs, someone said go to hospital and I left'

Wreford wrote her replies in his notebook and said, 'my officer here will record what you tell us about what happened and then you can go, but you will be needed for the Coroner and the Court, but we will tell you when'

Foster nodded and said, 'I'll tell what I knows but I left it was nothing I did'.

Wreford left the room and went to his office read over the statements that had been taken as they were brought to his office. He eventually was satisfied with all the evidence obtained. He stood up and walked to the cells where Kitts had since been placed following his outburst at Bennett's body. Kitts was brought from his cell by a sergeant and Superintendent Wreford said to him, 'I am charging you with causing the death of William Bennett a constable whilst in the execution of his duty.

Kitts said, 'is he dead'?

Wreford said "yes." Kitts then began to cry very loudly and said "we both fell over the stairs from the garret stairs; it was all that woman's fault."

Wreford then said, 'take him back to the cells and keep a permanent watch on him'.

Wreford then made his way to Kitts and Fosters room in Lower Lane to examine it for himself. He saw that there were broken ornaments and china on the floor and chairs were overturned. Blood could clearly be seen on the floor beside the remains of the china. It was plain to him that there had been a disturbance and an injury. He then went and examined the stair area and found fresh looking marks and scrapes on the plasterwork which were consistent with signs of a struggle on the staircase. He recorded these details, and returned to the Station House to ensure that everything had been completed for the courts, and to re-roster his officers to ensure sufficient cover for the next few days.

Chapter 17

PC Bennett's body was taken on a wheeled stretcher to the mortuary and placed on the marble slab in order that Sedley Wolferstan the Plymouth Borough Police surgeon could carry out his post mortem.

Dr Wolferstan smartly dressed and exuding an air of efficiency which couldn't be denied by anyone that knew him, arrived at the mortuary with his assistant early the next day, to avoid the heat.

The building itself was old and maintained a natural coolness from its sunless position which thankfully helped to preserve the bodies. This was particularly relevant considering the latest weather.

He wasted no time in putting on his protective gown, and stood beside Bennett's naked body which had been prepared by his assistant.

His first role was the examination of the body for obvious injuries and to record what he called a surface examination. This included the age, sex, the development, the colour and to look for obvious abnormalities.

Having satisfied himself that the frothing from the mouth was the only thing worthy of note externally he bent down opened his bag of instruments, selected a scalpel and quickly made two incisions.

These were made from each shoulder to the lower end of the sternum. Following this a single incision was made from where the two previous incisions joined to the pubic bone. When this was completed it had the appearance of being y-shaped, and his assistant then helped him retract the body skin and superficial muscles from the chest and abdomen thereby exposing the ribs and abdominal organs

This procedure they carried out was well practiced and standard in all his post mortem examinations. His assistant could anticipate his next move and was always ready with the instruments or receptacles needed to complete the examination.

The cartilage attaching the ribs to the sternum was then cut away and Dr Wolferstan passed the sternum to the assistant who placed it on a cloth nearby.

The heart was then cut out and carefully examined, weighed and Doctor Wolferstan made particular notes of his findings as he carried out this examination. The lungs and abdominal organs were then removed and examined in a similar manner.

The assistant placed a block under the neck in order for a scalpel incision to be made at the back behind the ears and the skin was pulled away from the top of the skull and face exposing the skull bone. The skull was then cut through with a bone saw, the bone removed, and Dr Wolferstan extracted the brain which he examined weighed and again recorded his findings.

When he was satisfied that he had completed all the necessary examinations to ascertain a cause of death, Wolferstan instructed his assistant to restore and stitch up the body. Whilst this was being carried out he monitored his assistants work but also made and rechecked his notes to ensure he had everything he needed particularly in relation to the heart and brain in order to present his findings to the Coroner and the Courts.

PC Bennett's body was finally washed and prepared for subsequent removal by the undertakers for his family to arrange his funeral.

The Coroner was informed along with the Police and as already arranged an inquest was held where the accounts from the various witnesses were heard, and the decision of the Coroner did not surprise anyone when he decided there was sufficient evidence for Kitts to appear before the Magistrates the next day Saturday 17th July.

Chapter 18

Saturday, the day of Kitts Magistrates hearing started early for Susan Foster. She had not slept well since the incident and spent most of her time, when not being seen by the Police, keeping herself away from her normal High Street haunts or staying in her room. She knew she was unpopular because of her association with Kitts, and many held her as being partly responsible over what had happened. Since Kitts arrest crowds had gathered in the street and around the Police Station letting their outrage known. News had spread fast within the High Street community and the local press had been quick to report the death and circumstances as best they could. Reporters found that, by talking to locals, they were able to gather all the local gossip and rumour, and there was plenty of that circulating; the couple were known in the area for their rows and drinking.

Susan's own background had made her used to appearing on

various charges but, this time, she was upset about what had happened and the prospect of appearing as a witness frightened her, she was involved in the death of a Policeman. She kept thinking about how easily a simple upset between her and Kitts had led to his death. She wished she'd kept her mouth shut, though she could not really remember exactly what she said, bits of it came back to her if she thought hard. It was all said in the heat of the moment. It all could have been sorted in an easier way; she had been hit before by Kitts, and others come to that. On some occasions she had fought back or even run away. She had been drinking that day was full of bravado and this had led to her shouting out - she should have kept quiet.

Susan felt frightened and intimidated by the whole incident and knew that facing the Magistrates was going to be far different; she had never been involved in anything as serious as this. No matter how hard she tried she couldn't stop thinking about it or put it to the back of her mind.

Susan had not seen her sister since the incident; she was obviously keeping low somewhere, and not wanting to get involved. This on top of her worries made her feel isolated and alone - she had nobody she could speak to and no support that she could easily call upon.

She lay on her bed in her room, still wearing her clothes. She was on edge and listened to every noise outside, each time she heard something she became startled and worried as to what it was. Her head was bandaged and still hurt if she laid directly on it. This was partly as a result of the injury and also because of consuming too much drink prior to the incident. She tossed and turned throughout the night, unable to sleep with thoughts about what would happen to her. Every time she almost drifted off to sleep her head was suddenly filled with nightmarish dreams about the incident and her forehead was wet with sweat. She now hated Kitts and realised her decision in hospital to take him back was her downfall, she should have been more sensible. In the early hours through exhaustion, she had drifted lightly off to sleep but was woken suddenly at about dawn. She woke with a start, sitting up straight and noticing it was starting to get light; she rubbed at her eyes trying to think what was happening hearing shouting outside her house. The memories of the previous day came flooding back and she immediately knew that it was to do with her and Kitts, and started to feel frightened. Groups of people had gathered outside early to demonstrate and make their feelings known. She could hear them shouting "Hang him; she caused it herself the whore." The mob in the street outside increased in number, along with the level of shouting, as more people found out what was happening and came to join them. As the crowd increased several broke away from the main group and started banging on her front door. Seeing this happen they were joined by others who started pushing at the door.

Susan's heart was pounding and she started to panic; she was glad she was dressed and thought to herself 'they are going to break in and get me'; she grabbed a scarf from the floor, and quietly opened the door of her room and carefully looked around the edge. She could see from the gathering daylight that the front door was being pushed and was starting to splinter and break away from the frame.

Driven by panic she ran to the back of the house and after several panicky attempts to undo the rusty catch of the door that led out into the small rear communal courtyard, she eventually slid it across and slowly, afraid to make any noise opened the door. She crept quietly across the courtyard avoiding where she could the decaying rubbish collecting on the ground. A cat suddenly jumped up from the rubbish to the wall at her approach, forcing her to stifle a scream with her hand. She reached up and grabbed the top of the small surrounding wall and pulled herself up - the fear in her seeming to provide extra strength in her arms. She pulled herself to the top of the wall, sitting and putting one leg after the other over - grazing her knees in the process - but biting her lip to prevent herself from making any noise. She dropped into the small lane, slipping on decaying rubbish as she landed - which caused her to end up sitting on the lane.

She kept crouched down for a moment, hurting, wanting to cry out in pain and rubbing her knees and licking the blood off her hands. The tears ran down her cheeks, she moved slowly along the lane in the direction away from High Street, stopping at the end to carefully look around the corners. She felt gradually more at ease as she got further from the house. It was fortunate she knew the area well having leant against many of the walls plying her trade. Walking as quickly as her sore knees allowed and using the scarf to partly cover her face and bandaged head, she hoped that she would not meet anyone she knew this early. Susan was breathing heavily and stopped, rubbed her knees this time with the scarf and managed to catch her breath before moving slowly on. Her heart was pounding and she felt scared but happier to have got away from the mob.

She stopped as the lane reached St Andrews Street, checking to see there was nobody about. She could see a few people walking, but there was certainly no mob shouting or looking for her in this direction. She wasn't sure where she was going to hide but turned left walking quickly with her head down and face partly covered towards Notte Street.

She was suddenly startled and jumped and froze when a voice behind said "Hello Susan where you off so early in a hurry, you in bother, I heard about your man?"

She hadn't noticed the person walking in the same direction but felt initial relief at hearing it was a woman's voice - which she thought she recognised. This curbed her initial reaction to run away. She slowly lifted her head and saw to her relief that it was Liz Elliot from the second-hand clothes shop in High Street.

She grabbed hold of Liz around the neck with both arms, burying her head into her shoulder and started to weep. "Oh, Liz I'm bloody scared, a mob was outside tryin to break in at me room, I got out the back, I'm bleeding."

Liz pulled her arms down and slipped her hands into hers, squeezing them, and said "You come with me lovie, I'm off to the shop, you can stay there a while till it all sorts, you'll be safe there."

Liz always had a soft spot for Susan, she felt sorry for her as everyone locally seemed to be against her. She knew what she did and her background following the death of her Mother and, in some way; felt she was a victim of circumstances. She had been a friend of her Mother and had this feeling that she should try and help her if she could. From their conversations in the past she knew that Susan had always wanted to better herself and one day leave her street life behind. Liz thought to herself there would be little chance of this now, but didn't say anything, as this would upset her even more.

They walked towards her shop and, as they turned into High Street, Susan moved close to Liz - keeping herself almost behind her - fearing that the crowd would come towards them and see her. She was relieved to see no sign of them other than a few people further away who seemed to be going about their normal daily business. There was no shouting to be heard, which eased her fears.

Once in the shop Susan hurried immediately into the back room where she slumped down in the corner on the floor; she examined her knees and saw that the blood had dried. She started shivering, and pulled some cloth she found nearby on the floor close to her body and hugged it to her. It was not the cold but fear that was causing her to tremble. She breathed deeply, gradually starting to feel safer now she was off the street, but how was she going to get to the court without the crowd attacking her.

The shop was not yet open and Liz had arrived early to parcel up some clothes for the workhouse which were being collected later. She could see as she busied herself that Susan was petrified and could see her keep looking around watching the doorway. She went over to her - bent down towards her putting a hand on her shoulder - and said "You stay put, I'll go up the street and see what's happening, nobody will take any notice of me being around, and I'll lock the door."

Liz returned, after what seemed a long time to Susan, and said "The Police came from the station nearby and broke the crowd up and they have been moved on, but I was told the Police are looking for you because of the court."

Susan said "I know, I'm supposed to be there, but I'll stay here till it's clear and then go; I'll ave to, will you come with me?"

Liz smiled at her, but didn't reply; she went to resume her packing in the shop, leaving Susan to recover and decide what she was going to do. Although Liz felt sympathy for Susan she did not want to be in trouble with the Police for hiding her, and knew she would have to leave soon.

The Magistrates Court, situated at the Guildhall, was due to start at 10.00am and as expected had attracted a large crowd of noisy locals. Rumours had spread like wildfire as to what had happened, with varying stories having been circulated in the streets and ale houses. The Western Daily Mercury reported that the story which held the most credence was that the policeman had been stabbed by Kitts on the stairs, kicked behind the ear by him in the street and then he had trampled on PC Bennett's body. This had ignited the interest of the local population, and the story seemed to gather new additions as it circulated.

As happened at most courts there were always the regular attendees in the public gallery. Some even saw it as a form of entertainment, and with the local knowledge regarding the volatile relationship between Foster and Kitts it was anticipated they would not be disappointed. There had been a certain amount of jostling and pushing by some to ensure that they got into court to watch proceedings.

Extra Police were present inside and outside the Guildhall, and the court fell silent and stood when the Magistrates, chaired by Mr Luscombe, the Mayor William Foster Moore, a local shipbuilder, and three other Magistrates entered the court.

The bench took their seats and the Chairman warned the crowd who had packed the court to remain silent during proceedings or he would clear the court.

Mr Luscombe cleared his throat, looked towards the crowded courtroom and said "Before we start the official business I think it would be appropriate for the poor widow of the Policeman to receive some kind of expression of public sympathy. I think subscriptions should be small because, as yet, we do not know what the Watch Committee will do. We on the bench have subscribed a guinea each and Mr Redford one of my

Magistrates has kindly offered to receive a contribution from the public."

This was met with nods and expressions of approval around the courtroom, particularly from the public gallery.

"Would you now bring the prisoner into court?"

The Western Daily Mercury - who were keen to report this story and had been following up every snippet of information published the story that day before the court proceedings and had described Kitts at the police station after his arrest as being *'a low type of humanity who was a miserable spectacle who sat cowering and restless on a chair trembling violently.'*

This description was not far out and there were gasps as he was brought in. Kitts was dishevelled, visibly weeping, and he stared down at the floor as he walked into the courtroom flanked either side by policemen. He stood trembling, didn't look around and leaned over the front of the dock as Mr Luscombe read and explained the charge of murder to him. His legs suddenly gave way whilst this was being read and the Chairman said "Kitts, you are obviously in a distressed state - you can sit down and listen to the proceedings." Kitts was grateful to sit down and sat leaning forward still trembling but listening intently to what was happening.

The first witness called was Thomas Kitto - a porter who lived at 3 Lower Lane; he had given his evidence at the inquest. His deposition was then read to the court by the clerk who asked if he had anything to add, he looked at the Magistrates shaking his head slightly as he spoke and said "The Policeman did not want to go into the house but the woman, Foster, was three parts drunk and said she would give the prisoner in charge and the Constable accordingly went into the house."

Kitto was dismissed by the Magistrates and left the witness box and sat at the back of the court wanting to listen to the remainder of the case.

Kitto looked towards the door of the court when William Smale, a carpenter, was called next; he had also given evidence at the inquest. After listening to his deposition being read out, he said, 'I saw a large crowd come from St Andrews Lane, and saw a policeman with Kitts and had heard the Policeman say "I am done." Smale looked down and tried to compose himself before speaking again and said in a shaky voice, 'I took the Policeman into a nearby shop where he was sat in a chair and given brandy but he died shortly afterwards'.

Smale was then released by the court but walked quickly out of the courtroom not wanting to hear any more; the incident had upset him, he had found it difficult to relate the story and wished he wasn't involved.

The clerk then said "Bring Susan Foster in."

This caused muttering in the public gallery as they eagerly awaited her appearance. They all stared intently at the door, waiting for it to open.

The court usher came back into court looking red faced and

bothered and said "she's not here and has not been seen."
Mr Luscombe then said "This is most unsatisfactory, I will adjourn the court whilst the Police look for her; the prisoner Kitts can be taken back to the cells."
On hearing this Superintendent Wreford, who was in the court, jumped up and left the room. He summoned two of his officers, briefed them and dispatched them to look for Foster. They first went to her address, without success, and then started looking around the High Street area and ale houses for her. They did not think she would be far away but was just trying to keep out of the way.
Liz Elliot had seen the police activity from her shop, guessed what was happening and said to Susan "They are looking for you I think, I will take you out in the street to them when they have gone on past a bit, I don't want them to see you here or for you to tell them."
Susan stood, she felt scared; she nodded, brushed herself

down with her hands, but said nothing in reply and clutched Liz's arm as she walked into High Street. They soon caught up with a constable and Liz told him that Susan had come to the shop and asked her to go to the court with her as she was scared of being attacked. The constable nodded and took hold of Susan's arm and walked her towards the court. Liz stood still and watched from a distance as the two walked briskly towards the court. She felt pity for her and knew she would be in for a rough time. She watched until they were nearly out of sight and heard some shouting from some of the locals as they walked past them. She knew they were not happy about the incident, and there were those that definitely blamed Susan for what had happened.

Chapter 19

Susan waited outside the court with the Policeman. She was nervous, kept her head down to avoid eye contact with anyone, and paced up and down – being watched carefully by an officer in case she tried to leave. The doors of the courtroom suddenly opened, which made her jump, as she was looking the other way, when a voice boomed out 'Susan Foster.' She walked into the court looking straight ahead, and was directed towards the witness box. She was more nervous than ever now and her heart was thumping, but knew she must say what she remembered.

There were murmurings and hissing from the public area as she walked by, but she ignored these, and the Chairman called the court to order.

She stepped up into the witness box still wearing the dressing on her head; the Chairman frowned at her and said "You were supposed to be here earlier today, where have you been?"

She said "My house was broken into by a mob earlier this morning and I ad to walk the streets since six o'clock."

"I see, well that's a matter for the Police, but as you are now here at last we will proceed."

The Magistrates Clerk stood, looked towards Susan and said "I will now read out the deposition you made."

I am a single woman and have lived with the prisoner as his wife at 6 Lower Lane for the last ten months; I occupy one room there. The prisoner works on the new railway at Tothill. Yesterday he went to work as usual at a quarter before six, and came home to dinner just after twelve. There was no quarrelling at dinner time. I next saw him at about twenty minutes past four; I had been scrubbing in the afternoon and I was at the Napoleon having a glass of ale which a woman had given me. I was not there two minutes before he came in and said, 'are you coming home?'

I said 'yes in a minute.' He went out and I followed him home directly. There were a few words then and he said I had no business over there drinking, and then he shoved me. My sister came in and he shoved me down again, and I think I must have struck the back of my head against the bedpost; it bled a little. The prisoner then smashed two or three plates on the floor he was not tipsy. I called out and my sister said 'what did you strike her for? If you can't live comfortably you had better part.' He did not strike me with his fist, but only shoved me'

The Clerk said "I will now ask you some questions and they, along with your answers, will be written down." Susan looked nervously towards him and nodded in reply.

He said "Did you fall on the fender?"

"No, if I didn't cut my head on the bed post I must have done it by falling on the shards of the plates on the floor."

"Did you not tell Superintendent Wreford last night that you fell against the fender?"

"Not that I remember."

"Were you sober?"

'I had had only two glasses of ale that afternoon and, not being used to it, it took effect. Often I don't drink a glass of ale a month."

This caused laughter and shouts from the public gallery, which made her reply difficult to hear, and the clerk said "What was your reply?"

"Sometimes I don't drink a glass of ale in a month. My head is bandaged because of the cut."

"Did you call out murder?"

"No, he never did anything to me to make me call out murder."

Susan looked down and then said "I never spoke to the policeman. I left the room and went to the ospital whilst the policeman was having the row with Kitts."

"Were you bleeding then?"

"Me ead was bleeding a little."

"Did you see the policeman?"

"I saw im come into the passage and go upstairs."

"What made him go up?"

"Because they said Kitts had gone upstairs. When I saw the policeman, I was standing at me own door."

"Where was the policeman then?"

"In the lane."

"And you spoke to the policeman?"

"I never spoke to the policeman."

"Who was in the passage alongside of you?"

"Oh, there was a mob."

"Who told the policeman Kitts had gone upstairs?"

"I don't know."

"Did you complain to the policeman of being ill-treated?"

"No, I never spoke to the policeman. I heard some little children in the street call out that he was ill-treating me."

Albert Jones, a retired man, was a regular at the courts. He spent all his time watching trials, and had become quite an expert at the procedures. He would always pride himself and take delight in explaining his knowledge to those less acquainted than himself. He had been sat listening and fuming quietly to himself at her answers, and could contain himself no more; he suddenly jumped up and shouted "Liar, I heard you say it, so did others in the street."

The Chairman said "Remove that man from court; you may resume your questions when he is outside. I will not tolerate a disturbance during such an important hearing."

Jones was led by a policeman from the court shouting "She's always drunk and a liar, don't listen to her." Jones was angry with himself for the outbursts, but he couldn't help shouting - he knew she was lying.

The Clerk waited for the man to leave, the door to close, and then said "Did you tell Mr Wreford last night that you complained to the policeman that the prisoner had ill-treated you?"

"Oh, yes I did tell him that Kitts had ill-treated me."

"Now did you tell him you told the policeman he had?'"

"Not that I remember."

Susan knew she had shouted out something to the policeman, but she couldn't remember what she said. She had drunk a lot before the assault, and it was all a blur - what with the fear and lack of sleep. Her mind was racing and she was thinking 'Am I trying to protect Kitts for some strange reason, I mustn't do it.' She didn't remember everything but they were making her look like she was lying, she was confused.

"Did you see the prisoner come down the stairs again?"

"No, I was gone to the ospital by that time."

"Will you swear you did not tell Mr Wreford that you made a complaint to the Policeman?"

"No, I can't remember speaking to the policeman. I was so flurried that I didn't know what I said."

"Flurried at your home or at the police station?"

"Both. I went direct to the ospital and, when I came back, the people were calling out about the policeman."

Susan raised her hand towards the dressing on her head and said "The surgeon at the hospital put lint on the wound at the back of me ead."

"Did you see the policeman go upstairs and collar the prisoner?"

"No."

"Did you see the policeman fall downstairs?"

"Oh yes, I saw the policeman and Kitts fall down the stairs."

"How many times did they fall?"

"Might be three or four. I did not see them begin to fall. I saw them fall from Mrs Glasleys. Between the scuffling they fell. As they fell the policeman had Kitts old by the collar. Someone then said to me 'you had better go to hospital' and I went. I didn't see them get up. They were scuffling down the stairs. I could see them from me door where I was standing. They fell from the second landing and were both down on their ands and knees crumped up."

"What did you say to the Policeman?"

"I didn't say I said anything to the Policeman"

"Did you tell the Policeman that the prisoner had threatened to murder you?"

"No."

"Did you tell Mr Wreford last night that he did so threaten you?"

"Not that I remember."

"You didn't call out murder?"

"No."

"Have you any wound except the one at the back of your head?"

"No"

"Were there spots of blood about?"

"Yes, a few on the floor and on the table."

"And in the passage?"

"No."

"Any on your clothes?"

"A little on my light garibaldi"

"Have you told the whole truth?"

"Yes, I have."

The Clerk then turned, bowed his head towards the bench and sat down.

Mr Luscombe the Chairman then said to Kitts "Prisoner have you heard what this woman has said?"

Kitts was pushed by the arm, stood and said "Yes."

Mr Luscombe then said "Do you wish to ask her any questions?"

Kitts looked towards Foster, who was looking away from him, and said "Yes I do."

The Chairman said "You will have another opportunity of doing so if you prefer it."

Kitts continued to stare at Susan and said in a loud voice 'I'll ask her a few questions. Last night when I came home from work I found her at the Napoleon drunk."

Foster quickly turned her head quickly towards Kitts and said "I was not" and looked away again.

"You were" and when I asked her if she would come home she said 'she would when she was minded to.'

"I didn't."

"When I came home there was no fire in and nothing to eat" - Foster was angry now and shouted out "There was a fire in and the place was scrubbed and nice when e came home." - She turned towards Kitts and waved her finger at him and said "You hadn't better say too much you know."

"What was in the house was your sister's?"

"Was not the bread and potatoes for dinner my own?"

"I'm talking about supper."

Foster looked down towards the floor and said in a low voice "The less you say the better."

'Kitts shook his head looked straight at the bench and said "This is not the first time she has done it your worships. I have tried her every way. I have coaxed her and marked her and walloped her, I'll tell the truth, yes I have walloped her but it's all no good."

The Clerk jumped to his feet and said to Foster "Has he ever coaxed you?"

Foster said "No, but not long since I was in the ospital with two broken ribs e gave me."

The crowd in the public gallery by this time were all sat on the edges of their seats listening intently to these revelations and whispering to each other, not daring to take their eyes off the proceedings.

Kitts immediately replied "Yes Sir, I did it. I'll tell the truth. She was drunk then too. When I came home there was no fire and I lit it whilst she sat in the corner. Then I sent her sisters child for an egg and gave her."

Foster said "I never saw it; you must have ad it yourself."

Kitts ignored her reply and said "When I gave her money to get some supper, she began playing and dancing about, and laughing at me."

Foster said "You didn't let me ave any money."

"Yes, I did, one and sixpence halfpenny, but you threw it back on the table."

Foster laughed and said "It's false; you might ave put it on the table. I went without myself, I always got is victuals. I ave pawned my things for im."

Kitts shook his head again and said "There was nothing in the house. She is always bad. I have tried to get a little home around her, but it's no good. She likes more men than one. That's it." He then sat down.

Foster was then asked to sit at the back of the court, and took a seat in front of the public gallery; she could hear the mutterings and feel the eyes on her from the hostile crowd behind.

Mary Williams, a widow who lived in the same house as Kitts and Foster, was then called and she told the court she had heard Foster say to the Policeman "I give him in charge see how he has cut me."

She described what she had seen of the scuffle between the

Policeman and Kitts and Mr Harvey assisting the Policeman. At the end of her evidence she said "Susie Foster did not call out murder or anything else, she called over for the policeman at the end of the lane, where he had stood seeing a mob collected. I did not hear all she said to the Policeman. I did not fancy that she was drunk. Kitts was quite sober; he is a passionate, but a very quiet and inoffensive young man and would do any good for anyone I believe."

This brought gasps from the public gallery and whispers could be heard amongst them, but the Chairman did not silence them. Williams was then told to leave the witness box and was directed out of court by an usher.

Thomas Harvey was then called to the witness box. He entered the box and, after taking the oath, he described himself as a shoemaker living at 7 Lower Lane.

The clerk said to him "tell the court what you saw on the night in question."

Harvey said "about seven o'clock I was in my room working when I heard a row and someone said the murder was being committed. I ran out and saw Kitts and Foster fighting in the lane outside their own door. Foster was bleeding very much from the head and Mrs Westcott, Fosters sister, threw dirt in the prisoner's face. Some men came into the Lane and they stopped fighting. They did not fight after that. Foster said she would have the prisoner taken up, and walked towards high Street, from which end of the Lane the policeman was approaching. She came in with him, and Kitts ran into the house the policeman close after him. The Constable did not see Kitts enter the house, but was told he had gone upstairs. Just after the deceased entered the house I heard a bit of a struggle, and gone upstairs. Kitts had the policeman down on the landing. As Kitts was all of a heap on the deceased, I hauled Kitts right off and said "policeman get up I'm right here."

The clerk said "I will now ask you some questions, "how did you haul Kitts off?"

"Oh, I Got hold of him where I could."

"Did you use any violence?"

"No."

"Didn't you choke him off? "

"Not then, that was in the Street afterwards. The policeman got up and walked downstairs first, Kitts followed and I came last. When outside I caught hold of the prisoner by the collar and wrist on one side, and the policeman on the other. Kitts went two or three steps and then fell."

"Purposely? "

"He made out to be in a faint or in a fit, and I unbuttoned his shirt collar. I said to him come on get up out of this. He then walked on quietly till we got to the corner of middle Lane in St Andrews Street, where he fell the second time." The policeman said "you had better hold him down" but Kitts replied "no, I will walk quietly." I said "wait we will give you one more chance and, if you don't come along quietly, I'll put you down quick and give you what you want." He said "alright Tom." But, we had not walked for five steps before the policeman said "I'm licked, I can't go any further." Kitts remarked "you go in policeman, and I will go on quietly with Tom here." "The policeman went into Barrett's butchers shop right and I went onto the station with the prisoner."

"Was there not a struggle in the Street?"

"No, the only thing was that Kitts in falling to the ground dragged the policeman over him. There was no tripping up or violence used after leaving the house."

"What did you mean by saying just now that you choked him off in the Street?"

"Well, when the prisoner went to the ground, once I thought he meant to kick out and so I put my arm on his throat to keep him quiet."

"You didn't see the prisoner throw the policeman down?"

"No sir."

"When you got up the stairs was the prisoner doing anything to the policeman?"

"He was in a heap in the corner. He was not moving or calling for help. He was jammed up, but I did not see any violence in the way of blows or kicks."

"What positions where they in?"

"The prisoner was on the policeman, and the policeman was jammed up in the corner with his head twisted round and his face on the ground."

"Was the prisoner kneeling on him?"

"I think he was kneeling on his bowels, I am not sure whether he was laying or kneeling on him."

"Was the prisoner sober?"

"Yes, he was sober, but Foster had been drinking."

"Do you know whether she spoke to the policeman?"

"She must have from what I saw."

"Was there any blood about Foster?"

"There were some on the back of her head, but I saw no wounds. The blood was about her hair and neck."

The Clerk said "Mr Harvey do you have anything further to add to your evidence?"

Harvey said "No sir, I've told you all I know, can I go now?"

Harvey left the witness box and smiled towards the gallery at the back of the court as he left.

The next witness called was Frank Twitchell who was the keeper of the Swan Public House.

Twitchell took the oath and the Clerk said "tell the court what you can remember about the incident."

Twitchell said "Right Sir, between 7 and 8 o'clock, I looked out the door and saw the prisoner and the Policeman going across the open space of ground near lower Lane. I saw the Policeman stumble and, thinking he may have been knocked down or dragged down, I went to see what was happening. By the time I got near them the Policeman was on his legs again and had hold of the prisoner by the arm. I noticed that the Policeman was panting heavily, but they walked on a few paces and I heard the prisoner say something about going on alone or something like that. The Policeman started staggering and said "I'm done for." I took him by the arm and placed him in Mr Barrett's shop, which is near to my place. It seemed to me as if he was death seized and turned the colour of a corpse. I said "where's your helmet" - he was gasping for breath and said "I don't know." I then ran and got some brandy; I came back and unbuttoned his tunic to relieve him as much as possible. He cried out "I am choking give me air." I and some others cleared people away from the doorway and somebody tried to give him the brandy but he couldn't swallow it and choked and started vomiting."

Twitchell was upset as he related his evidence and his voice was becoming more strained as he tried to control his emotions.

He looked at the bench and said "can I stop a bit to gather my thoughts and compose myself; I find it hard to talk about seeing a man die."

Mr Luscombe said "of course if you need to stop or sit for a while just ask."

Twitchell said "I will be alright now, I'll continue." The next thing that happened was that another Policeman who had arrived went off for a doctor, but no doctor came. The Superintendent and some other officials came shortly after, but he was dead before they came. He died within five or six minutes of being taken into the house.

Twitchell looked down and wiped his eyes with back of his hand and the Clerk said "is there anything else you can tell us?"

Twitchell said "the only other thing I can say is that someone in the shop asked the Policeman if he had been kicked but I didn't hear any answer, that's it."

He left the witness box and Superintendent Wreford took the

stand and told the court that PC Bennett had been with Plymouth Borough Police for a year and nine months. He had been working from 5 to 9 that evening, and that Lower Lane had been within his beat.

He then said "Having received information of this transaction at about quarter to eight, I went to the shop where PC Bennett had been taken but found him dead. I later at the station charged the prisoner Kitts with causing the death of William Bennett 'a constable' whilst in the execution of his duty. Kitts asked me 'is he dead'? I said "yes." He then began to cry very loudly and said "we both fell over the stairs from the garret stairs; it was all that woman's fault."

I afterwards went to Kitts house in lower Lane and found the room in a very disturbed state. Things were lying about broken and there was a quantity of blood in different places. The stairs showed signs of a struggle and the plaster was torn from the walls in several places."

The Chairman thanked the superintendent and said "we will adjourn to consider the evidence." The court rose and Kitts was taken back to the cells.

It was several hours before the Chairman and his bench returned to the court. During this time Kitts had been taken to the cells where he spent his time refusing food but pacing up and down. Susan Foster was made to sit outside the court and watched by a Policeman, and some of the crowd, who remained talking and airing their views in the vicinity of the court, but all keeping an ear out for the resumption. There was a rush of bodies back into the court to hear the verdict.

Kitts stood in the box shaking and looking down, not wanting to hear the Chairman speak.

The Chairman looked down at his bench towards his papers before looking straight at Kitts and said' there is sufficient evidence from the Coroner's inquest and this hearing to commit you to Exeter Assizes for trial, take him down'.

Kitts went weak at the knees and was held either side by Police officers who took him to the cells sobbing and protesting he had done nothing wrong.

Foster looked quickly around her and dashed out the door, not knowing where she was going to go; she just wanted to be away from people. She ran into the street and made towards her house pushing open the door running into her room where she pulled the table across the room and put it against the door. She sat on the bed panting and trying to catch her breath wondering what she was going to do. She would have to think carefully, she knew the Police would want her at the trial and would be coming to see her at some stage. She needed time to think and buried her head in the bed sobbing, thinking about that bastard Kitts, and listening for any noises outside. She had been laying on the bed for about an hour when she heard knocking on the door and a woman's voice shouting 'Susan, Susan'. She quickly sat up frightened, and then heard the woman say, 'it's me Liz

Elliot open your door quickly.'

Foster recognised her voice and jumped off the bed, pulled the table away from the door which she opened and saw Liz who said, 'I aint stopping there's nobody around at the moment but you need some help. You can stay in my shop out the back come out after dark; I'll be waiting for you'. Before Foster could reply Liz turned and was gone. The table was quickly put back against the door and Foster sat on the bed again feeling easier but wondering what was going to happen, she would talk to Liz as she felt sure she would know, and help her, but God knows why she thought.

Once it was dark Foster grabbed some clothes and belongings and left her room carefully looking outside and once she saw that it was quiet she made her way to Liz's shop. As she approached the door suddenly opened and she was grabbed by the arm and pulled inside, thankful to see it was Liz.

Liz took her into the back of the shop where she had stayed

previously and said, 'you can stay here until the trial starts, and just be careful when you go out. There is a back door you can use but its important nobody knows you are here'.

Foster said, 'what about the Police?'

Liz said, 'I've already thought about that, I've spoken to the Station House and told them I'm looking after you, they will tell me when you are needed, then they will take you and others on the train to Exeter, you will be alright then. I have also asked the Police to get in touch with Kitts railway friends and with them arrange for his few belongings to be removed from your room. The Police will lock up your room for you."

Foster started crying hugged Liz and said, 'I don't deserve none of this you is taking a risk for me, why'?

Liz said, 'you know I knew your Mother, before she left us, I said I would be there if I could help. Your father turned into a drunk and was away at sea most of the time, you was his favourite though when you were young and before he vanished, you could do no wrong. There were all sorts of stories about what happened to him but nobody really knows, things just haven't gone the right way for you. I got to tell you Susan that you have to change you will be dead early if you carries on. Once all this mess is sorted you needs to be away and sort yourself, that man has done you no good.'

Foster was sobbing uncontrollably as she listened, Liz was right if only things had been different and her parents had been there for her, but this wouldn't bring them back and she had to change. First, she must face the coming days, which would not be easy.

Being able to stay at the back of the shop for the time would help and Liz had said she would take her to the Police House when she was needed for the trial.

Chapter 20

The circumstances regarding the death of PC Bennett had incensed many of the Plymouth locals. In addition to the many expressions of public sympathy for his wife and family, there was a general feeling that it should not have occurred. The death of a Policeman on duty was something nobody had ever anticipated would happen in Plymouth especially during the arrest of a man for what was initially a domestic disturbance. The incident was of course the topic of conversation around the High Street and Barbican areas in the local ale houses, with numerous versions of what happened being discussed, circulated and in some cases changed considerably from the actual facts.

Superintendent Wreford had met with the Council and Watch Committee and it was agreed that Plymouth would honour the officer with a full civic funeral. This had been a popular decision and with the local feeling and outcry over the death along with the publicity it had received, he anticipated large crowds, so he detailed extra officers to cover the funeral.

Monday the 19th was going to be a sad day for many in Plymouth.

Just as expected large crowds gathered to pay their respects with many congregating in the street outside his house at 14, Hampton Street well before the start of the funeral procession. The streets leading to the gates and the grounds of the Plymouth Cemetery itself were also lined with mourners. It was later reported in The Western Morning News that as many as 7,000 people had turned out to show their respect, such was the feeling in the town.

The funeral procession formed outside his house just before 2.00pm. The undertaker Mr Isaac Foot of Hoe Gate Street ensured that everything was in order before entering the house to speak with Mrs Bennett and her family. The crowd fell silent and many bowed their heads in respect and openly wept as

Jane Bennett the widow, and wife of only a few months came from their house. She wore a long black dress, and a black shawl covered her head, but it was clear to see she was distraught and crying, though trying to be brave in the public glare, which was something she was not used to. She was supported and comforted by her husband's brothers and sisters who had travelled from the Landrake area.

Six sergeants of the Plymouth Borough Police acted as bearers and walked solemnly in front of the procession carrying the coffin which was draped with a wreath of purple immortelles. The family rode in two carriages behind.

Following the family was the Civic Party made up of the Mayor William Foster Moore and four Borough Magistrates accompanied by the Magistrates Clerk.

It was plain to see to all who attended this sad day that the large Police presence illustrated the deep impression it had made on them and the sympathy they shared for the loss of their colleague's life. They had all been shocked as to how a simple domestic incident had led to his death.

The Police procession was of course led by the Plymouth Borough Police, with Superintendents Wreford and Thomas at the head. They were followed by five inspectors, six sergeants, three detectives and sixty-five constables.

Next came two inspectors, three sergeants and thirty-five constables of the Devonport Borough Police which was the force he had first joined when he left home, before transferring to the Plymouth Borough Force.

A sergeant and eleven men of the Stonehouse Division of the Devon Constabulary followed behind.

The rear of the procession was made up of three warders of the Plymouth Borough Prison and three members of the West of England Fire Brigade. Plymouth had never seen such a funeral procession and it went slowly through the streets with many of the crowds deeply affected by the sight crying as the procession passed them.

The cortege reached the entrance to the cemetery and the crowds that had gathered were so dense that the bearers found difficulty making their way towards the chapel. The inside of the chapel was overcrowded and people had to withdraw to allow the coffin and mourners inside.

The service was undertaken by the Reverend Phillips the Curate of Christ Church, Eton Place, North Road, Plymouth, which was William and Jane's local church. It was a simple but moving service with many tributes being paid to his service and bravery.

Once the service was over the procession with the coffin moved from the chapel to the newly dug grave, but was held up as a portion of the side of the grave had fallen in as a result of the large crowds walking too close to its edge. This did cause an amount of consternation with the family over the delay, but they understood and appreciated the amount of support and sympathy that was being shown by the people of Plymouth, and how it had been caused.

The grave digger was called to widen it, and once this had been done PC Bennett was laid to rest.

The family and main mourners left the cemetery to return to Hampton Street, where many people still remained to pay their respects.

As the mourners reached Regent Street close to Hampton Street a bullock which was being held at the slaughter house owned by Newton's Butchers in nearby Tavistock Road escaped and ran in a wild state through the streets scattering numerous people along the way, but fortunately not injuring anybody.

Just as the cortege reached Regent Street to turn into Hampton Street the bullock ran towards the cortege, and as it did a brave Policeman ran at it grabbed a rope which was around its neck, pulled it and quickly tied the end to a nearby lamppost. This secured the bollock but caused it to become wilder enraged by the numbers of people. The group that had chased it from the slaughter house were unable to approach it for some time until it had settled and stopped kicking out. They then led it away to be slaughtered.

Fortunately for the family the bullock had run towards the cortege behind them, and apart from hearing shouting they did not witness the incident, and were able to return to the house to greet visitors and continue their mourning.

Chapter 21

Friday 23rd July 1875 a large crowd lined the streets of Exeter, eager to see the judicial procession which always took place on the first day, on its way to the Assize Court. The official opening of the assizes always attracted locals, particularly those with a curious nature eager to see the Judge and local dignitaries. Some people amongst the crowd were in awe of the assizes courts, through a fear of ending up there themselves on trial due to their activities, and would watch from the back of the crowd making sure that they were inconspicuous but had a weird sense of curiosity wanting to see others.

This was not the case with Albert Jones who was stood near to the castle entrance in a prominent position which would enable him to get a seat in public gallery and watch the trial. Although he had been thrown out of the Magistrates hearing in Plymouth for protesting at what he thought were the lies of Susan Foster, he was determined to see this trial. He had travelled up by train the previous day. The case had really fired his interest, he knew many of the people involved and anyway because of his regular attendance at courts he considered himself to be an authority on the law and court procedures. The assizes were held in the Devon Assize Hall known locally as the Castle. The building which had been finished about 100 years before had undergone numerous changes over the years. It had a stark appearance and many in authority liked to think this and the dignity of the formal procession helped to portray the might of the law, and would possibly frighten people to be law abiding citizens. There were also many that thought this was nonsense, and a few carriages containing men in wigs and robes weren't going to stop them and their life of crime. They had to live and took their chance, considering themselves cunning enough to avoid capture and the courts.

The presiding Judge Mr Justice Quain left the Judges Lodgings in his carriage resplendent in his ceremonial robes and wig, carrying his black cap which he wore only for passing the death sentence.

His carriage was escorted by the Mayor, Sheriff and various officials from the County and City. Either side of his carriage Police Officers carrying long staffs walked beside him.

He stared straight ahead during the ride and knew his time at this session was going to be long, having studied various court papers, but he felt ready to commence the courts business in dispensing justice as he always did.

His carriage arrived outside the Castle entrance and he alighted and walked to his chamber which was situated in a room behind his courtroom bench.

Albert Jones saw Superintendent Wreford enter the room, and watched with interest from his gallery front seat as the Grand Jury assembled in the court prior to the Judges entrance. He tried to identify individuals to himself, and noted with interest that the jury was chaired by the Honourable Leonard Allen

Addington, who he knew was the son of Viscount Sidmouth. He counted and saw there were 21 members of this Jury and he knew it was made up of men with a high social standing within the County such as mayors and magistrates. Albert felt pleased with himself and his knowledge, and looked at a man sat next to him and said, 'Do you know that the Grand Jury you see here is not the same as the jury that would try the case, a lot of people make that mistake.'

The man who had only come to the court out of curiosity tried to look interested, nodded and started to look away, but as he did Albert said, 'to continue what I was explaining, their role is to see that the prosecution established a proper case. They do this in secret and then at the end of their deliberations endorse the papers with 'True Bill' where a trial would take place or' Not True Bill' where there would be an acquittal.' The man smiled benignly at Albert as he finished the lengthy explanation but was not sure if he knew or understood what he had been talking about, besides he wasn't really interested and got up and decided to move to another seat that had just become vacant.

Mr Justice Quain entered the courtroom, having with the assistance of his clerk changed from his ceremonial robes and prepared himself for the proceedings, by putting on his court regalia.

The court rose at his appearance and the room became suddenly silent, people in the public gallery stopped talking, including Albert with many taking in the might of the law for the first time, but not so Albert Jones who had seen many trials.

The role of Mr Justice Quain was to charge the Grand Jury at the opening of the assizes and advise them on the cases, the current state of the law and any points he wanted them to consider pertinent to each case. He had a reputation for also using his opening address to advise them on the state of law and order within the County and to remind people of the need for education and obedience of the law.

Justice Quain arranged his papers ready to commence his charge, looked towards the jury and said, 'you must reach your verdicts with care. The calendar is probably a little heavier than usual in the number of cases and gravity of the offences, but there is nothing to show that the cases are of a very exceptional character.

The average number of cases at the assizes this time of year is usually 21, but on this present occasion we have 26. I have compared the calendar with that of former ones and there appears to be a little more violence than has been used in the County of Devon of late years. There are three persons in the calendar charged with wilful murder.'

He then outlined the case of Fowler a man accused of murdering his wife, paused and then said, 'The next case is one of considerable importance. It is the case of Kitts where a man is charged with murdering a policeman William Bennett at Plymouth while he was endeavouring to arrest him.

Albert Jones ears perked up when he heard the names and he moved in his seat leaning forward ready to take in all the minute details.

The case is a very peculiar one in its way, and Kitts has been committed on the charge of wilful murder.

A woman Susan Foster came out of a house where she lived with this man Kitts with her head bleeding, and on seeing a policeman near or meeting a policeman she said, 'Look how he has cut me; I give him in charge'

'Upon hearing this the constable went upstairs to take this man into custody, a scuffle ensued. No weapon was used but a scuffle, a very severe one, took place, the men fell down, the two together, several steps, and the first person who came in to interfere found the prisoner kneeling on the chest of the deceased.

The prisoner and the deceased then went out into the street; and there was the distinct evidence of one witness, a very important character, that he saw the prisoner take the constable by the throat or neck and throw him violently down.

It turned out that probably by the fall, there was no evidence of a blow being struck an effusion of blood came on in the brain and very shortly afterwards the man died, within a few minutes of the occurrence.

In this case the graver charge was a matter of question because as you are aware a Police Constable only has authority to arrest when he has reason to suppose a felony has been committed. A constable was not like a private individual, because with a constable it was sufficient for him to have reasonable grounds to suppose that a man was guilty of a felony in order to justify him in going to his arrest. Therefore, the question in this case for you to consider was whether he had reasonable grounds to suppose that a felony had been committed by Kitts in the intent to commit bodily harm on the woman Foster, and it becomes a serious question if the policeman has grounds for believing an act of felony had been committed, namely intending to do this woman bodily harm.

This is a case in which you will probably find your duty is to return a bill for murder and then these other questions can be considered afterwards.

The Judge then outlined various other cases to the Grand Jury and then sent away to undertake their deliberations.

The court was then adjourned and after the Judge had left Albert got up from his seat, but the man he had spoken to earlier had seen him looking towards him and hurriedly left the courtroom.

The Grand Jury as expected decided there was sufficient evidence to try Kitts on the wilful murder charge, and endorsed the papers with True Bill. Albert Jones could hardly hide his excitement at the prospect of the trial, which would take place on Monday 26th.

Superintendent Wreford hurriedly left the court knowing that his men would be busy arranging the witnesses and ensuring they all travelled by train to Exeter in time for the hearing. He knew the problems with some of them and he would make sure that his reputation was not tarnished in any way by the case not being presented in the right way. He felt he had a duty to the City, the force and to PC Bennett's family; he would not let them down.

Chapter 22

It was Monday 26th July 1875 and Justice had moved at a fast pace.

Kitts impending trial had caused great interest and the court was packed with members of the public including numerous reporters from the Plymouth newspapers and of course Albert Jones who had again managed to get a good seat in the public gallery. He was excited about the trial and as always anxious to impart his self-learnt legal knowledge on any unsuspecting person unfortunate to be cornered by him. With this in mind he kept looking around eager to select an unsuspecting member of the public.

Before the trial of Kitts there were two other short Plymouth cases to be heard by Mr Justice Quain, this was news to Albert Jones and he immediately forgot looking for someone to impart his knowledge to.

The first case involved Charles Smith aged 45, a coal porter who was indicted with feloniously wounding John Spargo at Plymouth on 30th March.

The prosecutor outlined the case by telling the court that at about midnight Spargo ran out of a house in Flora Street and accosted a police Constable on duty saying he had been stabbed. He had a wound in his throat and wrist which the constable bound. He identified Smith who was in fact his brother in law as being the offender, and he was taken into custody. It transpired that all the parties in this incident had been drinking, and Spargo was in the house in Flora Street when Mrs Smith came home and asked him had he seen her husband. He replied he had not where upon his sister did not believe him and took a fire shovel and struck him. He held her until her husband came home a few minutes later and the husband heard what had happened and began to assault his wife. Spargo took offence at his sister being assaulted and scuffled with Smith who stabbed him. At the police station a pocket knife was found on Smith and the wound on Spargos neck was found at the hospital to be 3 1/2 inches deep and 1-inch long. No other witnesses were called but Smith handed in a long-written defence in which he pointed out some discrepancies in the evidence he denied causing the cuts, saying that if he did so he would have been covered with blood and alleging that the blood stain on his knife was an old one.

The judge in his summing up said there could be no doubt that the prisoner stabbed Smith and the affair occurred during a drunken bout.

The jury were sent out to consider the evidence however to the surprise of everybody returned a verdict of not guilty.

The next case called involved a Plymouth woman Annie Winsor aged 38 who was indicted for marrying on 17th March 1872 at Plymouth one James Langdon a marine, her husband William Windsor then being alive.

Langdon and Annie Winsor were married at Sutton- on- Plym

Church Plymouth but it was afterwards discovered that she had married William Windsor at Exeter in 1860.

Winsor was questioned and said she had not heard of a first husband for years and it was because Langdon told her that he had seen a lawyer at Plymouth. He had said that she could marry if she had not heard of her husband for so many years. She therefore consented to marry Langdon with whom she had cohabited for some time previously. Now she said he had picked up with a woman who had money and wanted to get rid of her. His Lordship then called Langdon and said, 'why have you brought the case against the woman'

Langdon replied, 'because she had followed him about annoying him'.

Albert Jones who had been fascinated with this case could see that his Lordship did not appear happy and listened as he said,' I do not see that there is any evidence to show the woman knew Windsor was alive when she married Langdon and I direct a verdict of not guilty it was a shameful prosecution and should never have been brought before the court, I will adjourn for a short time before the trial of Kitts

The prosecution was undertaken by Mr Clark assisted by Mr Mckellar with the defence of Kitts undertaken by Mr St. Aubyn. Henry Kitts was brought into the dock from the cells below the court, handcuffed and between two constables and asked to stand. He felt frightened and overawed by the proceedings, but felt better than he did at the committal. He was surprised to see so many people in the court. He looked around for someone he knew a friendly face but could not see anyone. He thought to himself they were all against him anyway over what had happened so he should not expect anyone to have travelled the distance to support him. He knew that his only allies were his fellow workers who had supported him visiting him in prison. Mr St. Aubyn his defence barrister had seen him in the cells earlier and had explained the procedures of the trial and how he must behave. He must only speak in direct answer to questions, and not to shout out if he disagreed with what people said. He told him that his defence would be based on the policeman not acting in the execution of his duty.

The men of the jury had previously entered the court and sat in and stood around the jury box, waiting to see which 12 would be chosen from their number.

Everyone stood and went quiet when Mr Justice Quain entered the court; Kitts looked towards him and thought to himself that he looked very severe and an imposing figure in his robes. He could not help but notice the black cap that he carried, and tried to put those thoughts to the back of his mind.

The procedure of choosing the jury was carried out and the 12 chosen men were sworn in and their duties outlined by the learned judge.

The Court Clerk then turned towards Kitts and said 'Henry Kitts a labourer aged 24, in prison, you have been indicted for feloniously killing and slaying William Bennett, a Policeman of the Borough of Plymouth on the 15th instant and you are also charged on the Coroner's inquisition, how do you plead?

Kitts was looking pale and shaking when he heard the charge read out and said in a quiet voice 'Not guilty Sir'

Mr St Aubyn stood and said, 'My Lord I would like all witnesses other than Superintendent Wreford and Mr Wolferstan the surgeon to wait outside the courtroom'

His Lordship looked at the witnesses at the back of the court and said, 'Leave the court until called.'

Clark then rose to his feet, bowed, shuffled his papers turned towards the jury and said, 'Gentlemen of the Jury the prisoner at the bar Kitts is charged with the wilful murder of William Bennett, a Police constable of the Borough of Plymouth. It is a case of a somewhat peculiar nature, a case no doubt of the very greatest importance to the Police who should be properly protected in the execution of their duty, it is also a case naturally of paramount importance to the accused.

I shall state the facts and call witnesses to give evidence to support these facts, the defence will also have chance to cross examine any of these witnesses as of course does the learned judge. When all the circumstances have been laid before you, and you have heard my learned friend Mr St Aubyn for the defence and the summing up of the learned judge you must then come to such a verdict as you believe in your consciences would be right and proper.'

Clark then took a pace towards the Jury box, he slowly stared toward each of the jury members making eye contact, and said' it is for the prosecution to make out this charge, we must show that the policeman Bennett, at the time he came by his death was in the lawful execution of his duty. He must also have had reasonable grounds in believing that a felony had been committed when he arrested Kitts. Undoubtedly, he had no authority to arrest Kitts without a warrant, unless he had reasonable grounds for believing that a felony and not merely an assault had been committed. This will be a question of evidence for you to consider and after you have heard the evidence it will be for you to say whether Bennett had reasonable grounds for the belief that a felony had been committed or not'

Kitts had been listening intently to what was being said and kept looking straight ahead towards the prosecutor recalling what he thought had happened, he knew in his own mind that he had not intended to kill the policeman, but would they?

Clark then said,' the second point the prosecution must prove was that Kitts resistance caused the death of this poor unfortunate man. His Lordship will tell you that a party that resisted a policeman and killed him while he was in the execution of his duty was guilty of the crime of murder according to the law. We must also show that the policeman was in uniform and on his beat.'

Clark then lowered his voice and said to the jury,' With this explanation I will briefly lay before you the facts of this unhappy case'

Kitts put his head down staring at the floor, wondering about Susan, and what she was going to say, he had not seen or heard from her since his arrest other than today in court and when she was at the Magistrates following his arrest.

Clarke picked up some further papers looked at them and said, 'Henry Kitts the prisoner had been living in Plymouth for about ten months and was employed as a navvy by a contractor for the South-Western Railway.

The man whom he is charged with killing was twenty-seven years of age and had been with the Plymouth Borough Police for about one year and nine months. For some time, Kitts had lived with a prostitute named Susan Foster at 5, Lower Lane Plymouth. On the 15th July Kitts in order to buy some food obtained from his employer Mr Ralph, two shillings sub money.

He got to his home and found Foster was not there. He went out looking for her and found that she was drinking in the Napoleon Inn. A quarrel arose between them and whilst in Lower Lane he frequently struck the woman, one of his blows being so violent that blood flowed copiously from her head.

PC William Bennett who was on duty in uniform in the neighbourhood was called and seeing Kitts strike Foster he in answer to her demand proceeded to take him into custody for assault. Kitts at once attempted to make good his escape and ran into the house, the Policeman following close on his heels. Kitts rushed right up to the top of the house and had reached the garret door when he found Bennett close upon him. Both clutched and began to struggle. The landing was small and whilst holding one another the men fell over the stairs, the constable being under and Kitts on top of him. The prisoner then seemed to have got the upper hand for when Mr Thomas Harvey, a shoemaker residing in Lower Lane rushed up the first flight of stairs he found him kneeling on the deceased's chest. Harvey at once choked Kitts off and assisted Bennett to rise. When he got up the Constable true to his duty caught hold of Kitts on one side whilst Mr Harvey had hold of his collar on the other side, in which way the three walked down the stairs. Bennett did not relax his hold when they reached the street and walked on to the corner of St Andrew's Street. Noticing then that he seemed ill, Harvey told the Constable that he would take the prisoner to the Guildhall and immediately afterwards Bennett let the man go, and Harvey conveyed him to the Station House. Poor Bennett was then taken across the street into the shop of Mr Barrett a butcher, where he was placed in a chair and attended to by Mr Thorn, Mr Small and others. Mr Thorn asked Bennett if Kitts had kicked him, to which he replied 'No' adding that he could not breathe and that he was dying. Mr Thorn also gave him some brandy which he tried to swallow, but failed to do so, taking it into his mouth but bringing it up again. He hardly spoke another word and at about twenty-five minutes after seven quietly breathed his last. The body was taken on a stretcher to the Police station where it was examined by Mr Wolferstan a surgeon of the force. A post mortem was held followed by an inquest. I will now call witnesses.'

Kitts shuffled in his seat and gulped when he heard the name Susan Foster being called. He stared in the direction of the door hoping at least to catch her eye.

Susan had been given a dress to wear by Liz, and entered the court looking nervously around. She was directed towards the witness box and looked quickly towards Kitts, but then turned away from him when she saw him looking back towards her. She took the oath speaking in a quiet shaky voice.

Mr Clark said to her, 'tell me about yourself and describe where you live'

'I am Susan Foster a single woman and ave been living for the last six months with Kitts at 6 Lower Lane Plymouth. We only occupied one room downstairs; I was living with Kitts as his wife'

'Tell me about the Thursday and what you remember happening'

'He went to work as usual. Before he returned on this day I was in the Napoleon Inn, which is close by the house in which I live. I was having a glass of ale. Kitts came and saw me there and we had some conversation'

'What happened then?'

'At his request I went home just behind him'

'Tell the court what happened when you got home'

Susan looked towards the Judge and said 'We were in the room together when Kitts told me I had no business in this public house, and asked me why I had not got his supper. I told him I would get his supper, and on doing so he shoved me. At this time I was not intoxicated, but I was a little gone in drink, not being used to it.'

'Did he shove you again?'

'When he shoved me, I fell against the bedpost, and he shoved me a second time when I fell on the floor, and on one of the occasions I got a cut, not much, and a little blood came from it.'

'How did you get the cut?'

'I fell upon some shards of broken plates which Kitts had smashed by knocking them off the table, I did not cry out at all'.

'Was there anyone else there when all this happened?'

'My sister came in the room and said Henry, you ought not to strike her, and if you can't live comfortably you had better part. I had told my sister that he had struck me'.

'Did Kitts say anything then?'

'I am not certain of the reply he made, but knows that he and my sister went into the street and I followed.'

'Did anything else happen in the room before you go into the street?'

'I was much excited in the room and am not aware of anything taking place there beyond what I say'

'Tell the court what happened outside'

'In the lane my sister took up some dirty stuff and threw at Kitts, but I never imitated her in that respect. My sister said I would give him in charge and just then the Policeman came into the lane and I said I will.

'So, you told the Policeman you would give him in charge?'

'PC Bennett came over to my door and he must have heard me say I will give him in charge, I did not say that to the Policeman, I only said it to frighten Kitts, not meaning it.'

'Can you remember what happened next?'

Susan didn't reply immediately, shook her head, and said 'The policeman came through the crowd which had collected and someone hollered that Kitts had gone in the garret and the Policeman went up after him'

'Did you tell the Policeman you were bleeding?'

'Just as the Policeman entered the passage I said my 'ead is bleeding I will give him in charge. My head was not bleeding much, my head must have bled by reason of falling on the shards but I did not tell PC Bennett so'

'Did the Policeman say anything further to you?'

'Not that I remember I was excited by it all.'

'Did you see what happened next?'

'When someone hollered that Kitts had gone up stairs PC Bennett went up and from where I stood I heard a scuffle. When I saw them, they was locked together on the stairs, I went straight to hospital not waiting to see the end of it. When I returned from hospital they was all gone'

'Did you have blood on your clothes?'

'There was some blood on me garibaldi, nothing to speak of'

'Was PC Bennett in uniform?'

'The Policeman was in uniform'

'I want you to wait there; Mr St Aubyn will now ask you some questions'

Susan wiped her face with the sleeve of her dress looking

around the court; tears had started to well up in her eyes, she was frightened, and didn't want to talk any more for fear of getting herself into trouble. She knew she wasn't good at explaining things and wished the whole incident had not happened; it was not her intention for it all to end as it did. She blamed herself for shouting out and being heard by the policeman, it had all been caused by her anger, at least that's what she thought.

Mr St Aubyn said 'How did you get to the hospital and what happened there?'

'I walked down the hospital by myself and had me head dressed' She started crying again wiping her face, and said in a sobbing voice 'I beg your pardon gentlemen I hope you won't ask me anymore questions, I'm not fit to answer them I told you what appened'

Susan was now crying loudly and was bent over the witness stand.

Mr St Aubyn looked at Foster threw his papers down onto the bench, looked towards the Judge and said 'My Lord I have nothing further to ask this witness other than that she remains in court'

Mr Clark rose to his feet and said 'I also have no further questions and am in agreement with my learned friend's submission that she remains'

Mr Justice Quain looked at Foster and said, 'go and sit at the back of the court and do not leave until instructed'

Foster still sobbing hurried from the stand and rushed to the back of the court.

The next witness called was Mary Williams; she told the court that she lived in the same house as the prisoner.

Clark then said, 'on the day in question tell the court what you saw.'

'I heard quarrelling between Foster and Kitts. Foster came out of the house when the Policeman came into the lane and said to him, 'see how I am bleeding; I give him in charge'

'Where was she bleeding?'

'She was bleeding from the back of her head.'

'What did the Policeman do?'

'He went up in the garret to Kitts and then they fell down together on my stair-head. Kitts was on the Policeman and I called out from the window for God's sake come up or there will be a murder committed'

'What was Kitts doing?'

'He was kneeling on the Policeman'

'Do you know if Kitts had been drinking?'

'He was sober, and then Mr Harvey came up.'

'Wait there, Mr St Aubyn will now ask you some questions.'

Mr St Aubyn rose and said, 'You must have heard the Policeman say to Foster, 'you had better go and make him a cup of tea, 'this was after she said about giving him in charge'

Williams shook her head and said, 'No I never heard that said'

'Did you see any violence used by Kitts?'

'I saw no striking and nor did I hear any bad language used'

Mr St Aubyn looked towards Mr Clarke and said, 'I have no further questions'. Clarke stood and said I have no re—examination my Lord.

Thomas Harvey who along with Thomas Kittle and considered to be the two most important prosecution witnesses was then called.

He walked confidently into the witness box, took the oath and looked towards the barristers.

Mr Clarke said, 'would you tell the court where you live and what you saw on the night in question'.

'I live at 7 Lower Lane and on the evening in question I saw Kitts striking Foster, and heard Foster say, 'I'll have the blackguard took up'. The Policeman then came into the lane and Foster went towards him and said something.'

'Did you hear what she said?'

'I can't say what she said; but she came back with him to the door, she pointed to her head to the Policeman. She was bleeding very much and had been drinking.'

'What did the Policeman do then?'

'The Policeman went into the house, and up over the stairs, I heard a scuffle and ran up over the stairs.'

'Tell the court what you saw, take your time.'

'I found the Policeman and Kitts on the first landing, the Policeman under on his back with his head jammed up in a corner against the wall. Kitts was lying on him and I think he had hold of him. He was keeping the Policeman down so that he couldn't get up.'

'What did you do?'

'I hauled Kitts off and told the Policeman to get up.'

'Did Kitts use any violence towards you?'

'Kitts did not resist me'

'Did you see the pair scuffling?'

Harvey shook his head and said, 'I did not see them scuffling.'

'What happened next?'

'We then went downstairs, the Policeman first, and I last. When we got downstairs we collared Kitts, one each side. When we got three or four steps Kitts fell to the ground and dragged the Policeman with him.'

'What did you do?'

'I lifted Kitts up again and put my hands on his throat. I thought he was going to use violence. I goggled him a bit and he went off faint. He soon got better and I lifted him up again.'

'Did the Policeman get up?'

'No Kittle lifted the Policeman up.'

'Where did you all go then?'

'We went as before, 100 yards and then Kitts fell again. I told him not to play any tricks and he then said, 'I'll go quietly'. We went a few steps further and then the Policeman said, 'I'm licked, I can go no further'. Kitts said to the Policeman, 'You go and sit down, and I'll go quietly with Tom' meaning me, which he did. I walked on with him.'

Clarke said, 'you stay there, Mr St Aubyn will ask you some questions.'

Mr St Aubyn said. 'This is important; did you see any violence used by Kitts?'

'I saw no violence used by Kitts'

'Did Kitts throw the Policeman on the ground?'

'No, nor did he throw the Policeman down.'

'You were the only one who used any force, on Kitts in fact?'

'I did choke him a little but when he goggled I let him go.'

Thomas Kittle was then called, Mr Clarke said, ' can you tell the court your occupation, where you live, and what you saw on the 15th July.

Kittle said, ' I'm a porter and live in 3 Lower Lane and was home on this occasion. I heard a noise and looked over my window. I saw Kitts and Foster and her sister I saw them both pitching refuse and heaving dung at him. Soon after the prisoner went into the door of the house, the policeman came round the corner. Kitts was out of sight before he came. Foster's sister said, " go and give him in charge', and Foster went and met the policeman and twice said, ' I give that man in charge for ill using me ' she was covered all over with blood'

Foster who had been sat listening intently to what was being said suddenly jumped from her seat and screamed out, ' it's false I was not covered with blood it's false'

The judge leaned forward on his bench and said, ' put that woman out of court, give her a seat outside'

A court usher took hold of Foster by the arm and led her from the court still shouting and told her to sit by the court door and not to move away unless instructed.

The judge said, 'you may resume now Mr Kittle'

Kittle said, ' the Policeman and Foster then went into the house together and soon after I heard a woman cry out the window 'for god's sake come up they're murdering the Policeman'. I ran into the lane and just as I was going to enter the door the policeman jumped down two or three bottom stairs landing in the passage. He was followed by the prisoner and Harvey next. They came out into the lane and they walked four or five steps when he threw the policeman taking him by the collar and throwing him over his knee. The policeman pitched on his shoulder with Kitts on top of him.

Mr Clarke said, 'Did Harvey have hold of Kitts?'

'Harvey was close by but had not got hold of him, I am quite sure of this.'

His Lordship said, ' are you sure about this? '

Kittle said, 'yes'

His Lordship said, ' where was Mr Harvey all this time?

Kittle said, ' he was on the left of the prisoner. '

Mr Clarke said, ' was he holding him?

Kittle said, ' I don't believe he had hold of him'

Mr Clarke said, ' he fell on the ground I suppose'

Kittle said, ' yes the policeman upon him'

The judge looked quizzically towards kittle and said, ' are you quite sure about this?'

Kittle said, 'yes'

His Lordship said: ' Harvey says he caught hold of him the whole time and nothing of the kind you speak of occurred'.

Kittle looked at the judge and said, ' I don't believe he had hold of him until he assisted the prisoner up. He had hold of him all the time afterwards. The prisoner went off feint and crying, and on recovering Harvey had hold of him all the time. They went out the lane together'

Clarke said, ' Will you wait there please '.

Mr St Aubyn, stood and said to Kittle, ' did you not hear the policeman say to Mrs Foster, ' you had better go in and make a cup of tea for him'

Kittle said, ' yes I forgot that'

Mr St Aubyn said, ' that was after she said she would give him in charge? '

Kittle said, ' yes'

Mr St Aubyn said, ' immediately after? '

Kittle said, 'yes'

There were no further questions from Mr St Aubyn, Mr Clarke, or the learned judge and Kittle was asked to remain at the back of court.

William Richard Smale was then called by the Crown and told the court that on the evening in question he saw large crowd coming up St Andrews Street.

Mr Clarke said, 'Did you hear the Policeman say anything?'

'I heard the policeman say, ' I can go no further, I am done up, I'm licked '. Kitts then said, 'all right Tom I'll go with you and went with Mr Harvey.'

'What happened to the Policeman?'

'I went with him into Mr Barrett's; we placed him in a chair and gave him a little gin and brandy. He appeared to be very weak and in great pain, and frothed at the mouth.'

Smale looked down and hesitated, and said, 'shortly afterwards he died.'

'How long were you there with the Policeman?'

'We were in the shop about five and twenty minutes'

Clarke said, 'would you remain there my learned friend Mr St Aubyn may wish to ask you some questions'

Mr St Aubyn rose and said, 'Did you talk to the Policeman?'

'I had some conversation with him; I said have you been kicked? He said no kick I am choking, and then shakingly said I am dying, give me air.'

Mr St Aubyn then said, I have no further questions and sat down.

Clarke rose slightly, turned the judge and said I have no further questions of this witness.

Smale left the box with his head bowed and remained at the

back of the court.

Superintendent Wreford was then called from the back of the court.

Mr Clarke said, 'Tell the court about Pc Bennett and what you did on the 15th July.

Wreford reached into his jacket pocket and removed his note book and said, 'Pc Bennett had been a member of the Plymouth Borough Force since November 1873, having previously been in the Devonport Borough Force. On the night of his death Lower Lane was part of his beat. I saw PC Bennett dead at the station and he had froth all over his mouth. I later charged Kitts with causing PC Bennett's death whilst in the execution of his duty, and he said, 'we both falled over the stairs together from the garret stairs, it's all that woman's fault.

I afterwards went to Kitts room and found it in a state of great disorder, there were ornaments broken and blood about. In the stairs there were signs of a struggle.'

Clarke sat down and St Aubyn rose and said I have no questions of this officer.

The police surgeon Sydney Wolferstan was then called to give evidence.

Clarke said, you are experienced in court matters will you tell this court about the death of Pc Bennett'

Wolferstan studied the papers he held and said, ' I was called to the Guildhall and saw the body of the policeman. He was quite dead, and the body was lying on a stretcher a great deal of froth was about the body and the stain of brandy on his shirt. I made a superficial examination then but was unable to discover the cause of death. The next day I made a post mortem examination of the body'

He looked up and said, 'There were no external marks of violence to the body. I examined all his internal organs and found them healthy with the exception of the heart, which was considerably enlarged and one set of its valves were thickened and the blood vessel close to it degenerated. I then examined his head and found no injury to the skull or to the bones. On the surface of the posterior part of the brain on both sides there was a considerable effusion of blood. The effusion was in my opinion sufficient to cause death, and may have been caused either by a fall on the back of his head or by a blow without any external injury. His heart had nothing to do with his death I think. '

Clarke said thank you Dr Wolferstan.

Mr St Aubyn jumped to his feet and said 'you say Dr that in your opinion the cause of death was effusion of the blood in the head'

Dr Wolferstan said, 'yes'

Mr St Aubyn then said, ' might not that effusion have been caused naturally? '

His Lordship interrupted and said,' what you mean by naturally?'

Dr Wolferstan said, ' I understand the question to me was, might not the effusion have arisen from disease? '

Mr St Aubyn said, 'Yes, I mean might not the effusion have arisen naturally as the result of disease, apart from any fall or blow? I mean what is commonly called apoplexy'

Dr Wolferstan thought for a moment and said, ' before people have apoplexy they are not subject to a choking sensation, or foaming at the mouth, or want of air'

Mr St Aubyn said, ' when people are taken with fits of apoplexy don't they get such sensations such as foaming at the mouth? '

Dr Wolferstan said, ' no, those are not the preliminary symptoms'

His Lordship leaned over his bench towards Wolferstan and said, ' does not apoplexy result from some rupture?

'Wolferstan replied, ' yes my lord a small rupture'.

Mr St Aubyn said, ' might not the rupture have occurred in the baker's shop? '

Dr Wolferstan said, ' no I think not'

Mr St Aubyn said, ' no I know you think not. But supposing you had been called into the shop to see him, had not heard of the scuffle at all, might you not have ascribed death to have risen from apoplexy? '

Dr Wolferstan nodded, looked towards the judge and said, ' the policeman was probably too young for his death to have probably arisen from an apoplexy. '

The judge said, ' you don't think the deceased died from apoplexy? '

Dr Wolferstan said, ' I think not. In case of disease the blood would probably be found in the substance of the brain and not on the surface.'

Mr St Aubyn said, ' I need hardly ask you if the man had fallen over the stairs if they would there not have been some marks on his body? '

Dr Wolferstan shook his head, and said, ' not necessarily'

Mr St Aubyn said, ' I mean the possibility'

Dr Wolferstan said, 'possibly but not as I said necessarily.

St Aubyn frowned, looked through his papers and sat down.

Mr Clarke then jumped to his feet, bowed to the judge and said,

' My Lord that concludes the case for the prosecution'

Mr Justice Quain, nodded slightly towards Counsel, and said, 'I think this is a convenient moment for a break before I hear further matters', he stood and left the court.

Chapter 23

Everyone remained in the court with the exception of the Jury who were escorted to their room and Kitts who was taken to the cells, and glad to leave the heavy atmosphere of the court. Foster kept her head down and didn't want to talk to anyone. She was frightened, didn't want to be there and was wondering what was going to happen when the Jury eventually made their decision. She knew she wasn't popular and if Kitts was convicted she would need to make a hasty move from the area, but she thought where the hell can I go without money. She also wondered what would happen if he wasn't convicted, that would also be a similar problem for her. She felt alone and didn't have any support or someone she could talk to in the court. She felt it was best if she just sat still, kept her head down, knowing she would have to move quickly from the court at a later stage of the trial, regardless of the outcome.

The public gallery with of course Albert Jones now brimming with his knowledge was buzzing with conversations and opinions. He tried to engage people with his views but most were content to let justice take its course and not want to know his opinions. There was though certainly a division in the predicted outcome of the case, but the result would not come yet as further

It seemed a long half an hour before the Jury and prisoner Kitts were brought back into court.

The court rose as his Lordship entered and Mr St Aubyn remained on his feet and said, ' My lord I would like to make a submission that there is no case to go to the Jury in relation to the charge of wilful murder, my submission is quite simply that Bennett was acting illegally in attempting his arrest and had no grounds to do so. I do not wish to add any more to this submission, but it is plain to see from the evidence.' St Aubyn sat down and Justice Quain looked at Clarke, and said, 'what have you to say about this submission?'

Clarke said,' My Lord, there is not a lot I can add, the evidence as we have heard today clearly must show that the Policeman had reasonable grounds for believing a felony had been committed and therefore acted legally in making the arrest. I can add nothing further there was violence used and the incident resulted in the death of the Policeman.

His Lordship consulted his notes, asked both counsel to stand and said,' I have listened carefully to the evidence given by the witnesses and must rule in favour of Mr St Aubyn, and the case must proceed on the manslaughter charge only. I will advise the Jury later in my speech, but members of the Jury you must consider the evidence only on the manslaughter charge the charge of murder has been dismissed.'

This caused gasps and a ripple of conversation from the gallery and his Lordship looked up from his notes, and stared towards the gallery, which was all that was needed to maintain silence in his court.

Kitts put his head into his hands and struggled to keep his emotions in control.

Foster kept looking down with her mind racing, trying to think what she would do trying to plan an easy way for her to avoid any contact.

Clarke rose and waited whilst his Lordship finished writing his notes and said,' I have been relieved of a great responsibility, and accept your learned judgement, I will now address the Jury in support of the charge of manslaughter'. He turned towards the Jury and looked straight at them moving his eyes along their bench as he spoke. 'I submit that there is a case of manslaughter for you to consider against Kitts. The evidence you have heard clearly proves that Kitts did use unnecessary and unreasonable violence in the manner in which he struggled with the Policeman on the stairs. You have heard from Mr

Harvey that the officer was found lying on the stair landing with his head jammed in a corner and Kitts kneeling on top of him. Harvey had to choke him off. I accept that there is contradictory evidence with regards to the affray in the street but by Mr Kittles account there undoubtedly was violence used. I submit that there is a case to answer in relation to the charge of manslaughter, and that you should find Kitts guilty of this offence. You must consider the violence used and the resultant death of PC Bennett. Kitts is guilty of the offence of manslaughter without any doubt.' He held his gaze towards the Jury for a few seconds before sitting down.

Mr St Aubyn rose slowly, adjusted his gown over his shoulders and picked up his bundle of papers and said, 'Members of the jury you must like me be equally relieved that the charge of murder has not to be tried. I feel sure that the charge of manslaughter will also fall to the ground. What are the facts of this case? Kitts and the woman Foster, who is sat at the back of court, had a quarrel as persons in their station of life often did. That quarrel was aggravated by other people interfering and making mischief. Kitts did not seek a quarrel but when the Policeman came along and was spoken to he tried to get out of the way. Then when he was followed and an illegal attempt to arrest him was made, he did what everyone who calls himself a man would do he resisted. In that resistance it should be remembered no blow was struck, no weapon was used. There was a struggle and the parties fell over the stairs, and in that way the unfortunate Policeman came to his death by misadventure and by misadventure only. With his dying words PC Bennett has exonerated Kitts from the charge of killing him, or using undue violence.'

St Aubyn paused looked at the Jury and said,' I feel that with these facts you will also take the merciful view. No doubt if Kittles version of what had taken place was correct, Kitts would be guilty of manslaughter; but the evidence on that point is very contradictory and be reminded members of the Jury that the prisoner is entitled to the benefit of the doubt and therefore you must acquit him.

He stared towards them to emphasise his point and then sat down.

Mr Justice Quain then turned towards the jury and said, ' gentlemen of the jury I now have the duty of summing up the evidence in order for you to make your decision. The question of wilful murder having been disposed of, the sole remaining question is whether the prisoner is guilty of manslaughter, and whether in resisting arrest he was guilty of such unreasonable and excessive violence as to cause the death of this man.

It is not because the policeman was wrong in the first instance, in attempting to arrest him, that excessive and unreasonable violence should be used. I think it is well you, and indeed everybody else, should understand the point upon which this case turns, and before I go into the evidence it may be useful for me to explain to you the grounds upon which I came to the conclusion that the charge of wilful murder must fall to the ground. The law on this subject is well understood.

It makes a great difference between an arrest by a private individual and an arrest by a police Constable. It makes this great distinction between the two that whereas a police constable may arrest if he has reasonable grounds for believing that a felony has been committed, a private individual can only arrest in cases of a felony having been actually committed, a very different state of things.

The officer whoever he is who arrests must have at all events a reasonable and sufficient ground to do so before depriving that person of his liberty. Now arresting a man which I am sorry to say is not an uncommon occurrence should always be considered a very serious and important matter. It involves taking him into custody before the face of the public, and carried probably along the street in custody, which to some men would be infinite disgrace and dishonour, and therefore before an officer takes upon himself to arrest a man he ought to be well assured and has authority to do so.

Of course, if a felony is committed in his presence, if even there was only an assault committed in his presence, but there is a reasonable probability that the assault will be renewed, the policeman should interfere and arrest without a warrant.

In urgent cases where there is a probability of a man escaping, for instance, or anything of the sort, a police officer necessarily interferes and does not wait for a magistrates warrant to enable him to do so. But I fear from what I've seen that police officers as a rule are a little too ready to arrest people on all occasions. They seem to think that arresting a man is almost their first duty. It is the first thing that occurs to them. But I wish to impress upon them that that is not the first duty, excepting in cases of extreme urgency. If a crime is committed in their presence, or an assault which is likely to be renewed, let them interfere by all means, but if they had no knowledge of the crime themselves they should be well assured and have good evidence of it before they arrest the person at all, especially in cases like this where the felony or the simple misdemeanour is so difficult to distinguish by anybody who is not there, and does not know what is done.

Blood may be produced by a simple assault, but it does not follow that grievous bodily harm was intended, or the consequences of the assault would be dangerous. In that classic case it would be far better for the police, unless there is some very urgent ground on the contrary, to take the person so assaulted before a magistrate, swearing information against the offender, and then arrest him in the regular way by magistrate's warrant.

In my judgement there was not in this case sufficient ground for supposing that a felony had been committed, that is, that the man wounded the woman with intent to do her bodily harm. The mere fact that the woman had some blood on her head and jacket and that she told the policeman in an excited drunken way that the man had ill-used her, was not sufficient and reasonable ground, in my opinion, why the policeman should have acted in the violent way he did when he tried to take this man into custody. There was not the slightest prospect of a renewal of any violence, for the woman had actually walked away to the hospital to have her head dressed, and the disturbance was all over. Indeed, it should be recollected that the policeman advised Foster to go in and make a cup of tea for Kitts and make up; that there was no prospect of a renewal of any violence was proved by the fact that Foster walked to the hospital.

I think it right that you should distinctly understand the law upon this subject, and that that this is the reason why the charge of wilful murder falls to the ground.

We now come to the charge of manslaughter. The prisoner must be shown to have used unnecessary or excessive violence in resisting. A policeman in uniform was entitled to some respect and could not be resisted to the same extent as a private individual.

Assuming that Bennett even had no right to make the arrest there was no reason why excessive violence should be used towards him.

I want to draw your attention especially to the evidence of Williams and Harvey with regard to the position of the policeman and a prisoner on the landing. Was there any necessity in resisting the policeman and Kitts should kneel upon him and keep him down? It is for you to consider whether merely in resisting arrest such an amount of violence was justified. It was a reasonable fact that no weapon appeared to have been used and no blow to have been struck. There was very remarkable contradiction between Harvey and Kitto as to what was alleged to have occurred in the Street. No doubt both witnesses were equally honest in their statements and you the jury will have to draw your own conclusions. If the prisoner did throw the deceased in the way that had been described by one of the witnesses, there was no justification for anything of the kind, and if he'd caused or accelerated the death of the policeman, the prisoner ought to be found guilty of manslaughter. Members of the Jury I now want you to go to your room and consider the evidence in relation to the charge of manslaughter'

Chapter 24

The jury filed out of the court and Foster wriggled uneasily in her seat, not sure what to do, she had to wait for the verdict in order for her to decide.

She needed money and had an idea as to how she could possible deal with this but she needed to return to Plymouth first. She kept her head looking down not wanting to make eye contact or talk with anyone.

Mr Justice Quain looked around the court, examined his papers and referred to his clerk regarding further court business and matters that could be dealt with in the absence of the Jury. He was about to adjourn for a short recess when the court door opened with a crash and the Jury clerk entered, looking flustered and red in the face. He stood in front of the bench and faced the judge. Eventually his Lordship looked towards him with a frown and the clerk said, 'my Lord a verdict has been reached'
.

The Jury had been out for about five minutes and the clerk was ordered to ask them to return to the court along with the prisoner Kitts.

Whispers could be heard amongst the people in the public gallery speculating as to what would happen next and Albert Jones was quick to tell everyone that he was guilty, there was no doubt about it.

Kitts was brought from the cells and was made to stand handcuffed between two custodians. He was shaking and his tear stained face was white as a sheet. He stared ahead looking towards the judge.

The jury members some looking towards the floor, walked back into court and nothing could be guessed from their faces. They filed slowly into the jury box and took their seats. The court clerk asked the foreman to stand, and said, 'have you in relation to the charge of manslaughter reached a verdict to which you all agree?'

The jury foreman, looked towards the bench and said, 'yes not guilty'

Kitts fell to the floor of the box sobbing and was helped to his feet, the court erupted into shouts and cheering which incensed his Lordship, and he banged his gavel several times on the bench shouting, 'silence in my court'

The noise stopped immediately but there was confusion mixed with some disbelief on the faces in the gallery.

Jones looked flabbergasted and didn't want to speak to anyone and quickly pushed his way quietly out of the gallery.

Foster wasted no time, rose and hurried out of the door where she was stopped by a police officer, who said, 'you stop here, you aren't going anywhere yet till the Superintendent has spoken to you'. She was made to sit on a bench.

Mr Justice Quain looked at Kitts and said, 'you are free to go'

Kitts was taken to the cells returned his property and released to join several of his railway colleagues who had been in court. They walked from the courtyard of the building shouting and laughing heading to the station to return to Plymouth to celebrate in the High Street area.

Foster was told she would be escorted back to Plymouth on a later train so she could avoid Kitts. She had made up her mind that he was not going to be part of her life, but there was something she had to do when she returned.

Chapter 25

Susan Foster couldn't wait to leave the train in Plymouth, and pushed her way past people anxious to avoid the chance of conversation or verbal abuse.

On reaching her house in Lower Lane she found the front door unlocked and once inside she found the door to her room was damaged and easily opened.

No doubt despite assurances it would be kept secured, someone had been into her room. There were still a few of her already meagre belongings there, which had been scattered around. She was relieved to see that there was no actual damage but a search of sorts had been made, but she was not worried at that stage as she had plans to change her life and move on once she had some money.

She also realised it may have been her sister who had been in the room, but she didn't want any contact with her, as she had avoided her since the incident.

The main thing that Susan could see was that the bed hadn't been moved, and hopefully they hadn't found what she was desperate to get her hands on.

She pulled back the bed and smiled to herself when she saw that the small section of loose floorboard hadn't been disturbed. She prized it up with her nails and reached in and retrieved the silver coloured locket, and held it in her clenched fist. It had been a few days since she had taken it from the neck of the collapsed man off High Street, and the time was now just right for her to try and move it on for money. She felt that now her luck was in. Ironically that all could have changed if Fishy Mick had not met a sudden end.

She would have to go without food that night but in the morning, she felt sure the locket would make her some money. She dragged the bed towards the door and put it at an angle so that the corner was jammed against the door.

She didn't sleep well listening and clutching the locket, but she knew she would need to be up early.

Susan rose whilst it was just getting light and cautiously made her way out into the cool early morning air still clutching the locket. She walked slowly into the High Street keen to avoid people.

There was a merchant shop in the High Street which although dealt mainly with rags, Foster knew from previous encounters was not averse to buying items with not too many questions asked providing it was of some reasonable quality.

She knew that it opened early and was pleased to see it was quiet with just the owner inside sorting bundles of old clothing, she was still clutching the locket.

Susan approached him, startling him at first as he had his back to her, and said, 'will you ave a look at this its silver or something and is worth some money if you can buy it from me'

He scowled and said, 'where did you get this from you've caused enough trouble in this area lately I hope it's nothing to do with that, cause if it is you can shift your ass quickly out of ere'

Foster said, 'no it aint, honest mister I was given it by a seaman who didn't pay me for pleasure but told me it was worth more than what I had given im the ungrateful bastard'

He took hold of the locket and said, 'you better be right'. He tore off a piece of rag and rubbed the face of the locket, and inserted his long dirty thumb nail into the side of the locket which split in two. He squinted at the inside of the locket and said, 'there's something scratched on the inside it looks like 'Foss'

Foster felt the blood drain from her face and said, 'what'? She grabbed the locket from his hand, saw the wording and screamed uncontrollably falling to the floor sobbing, and shouting out, 'no no, what ave I done'

The instant reality dawned on her that the man who had collapsed and died off High Street, who she had taken the locket
from was her Father, who would always call her Foss.

The owner shouted out, 'what's wrong with you, you're causing a disturbance here which I don't want, the police or someone will be wondering what's happening. Take the locket and get out,
are you mad or something.' He took her hold by the arm lifted her up and pushed out through the open door onto the street where she slumped to the ground. He quickly closed the door and locked it.

Foster lay on the ground clutching the locket sobbing. How long she laid there, or what happened next, or who found her is unknown.

The last that was known of Susan Foster was that she was a resident in the local workhouse. The heavy burden of Bennetts death and the discovery she had robbed her own Father had played heavily on her mind and severely affected her mental state.

Chapter 26

The incident and resultant acquittal of Kitts had caused great consternation in the Plymouth area, particularly High Street. Most people felt there was an injustice and were blaming Susan Hooper for being the cause of the melee that led to the death. The editor of the local paper was very aware of the unrest and wanted to provide a balanced view of the events and eloquently summed up in his interpretation which provided the locals with a fitting tribute to their Policeman.

Nobody can read the report of the trial of Henry Kitts at Exeter, for the murder of the Policeman Bennett in Lower Lane Plymouth, without perceiving the importance of the legal issues which the case raises.

The protection of the police is a matter which has often been gravely considered, and there can be no doubt that powerful measures are necessary to prevent outrages, the perpetration of which casts contempt on all authority. Hitherto the West of

England has been free from those crimes which have won for the Northern Counties so unpleasant a notoriety for violence, and it is certainly to be hoped that the case investigated may not prove the forerunner of others of its kind.

Kitts action was by no means warranted, and if there was testimony as to the direct intention to violate the sanctity of human life which is usually regarded as necessary before a jury will bring a verdict of wilful murder, there was clearly in Lower Lane a disgraceful struggle. Moreover, Kitts was perfectly sober when he was the occasion of Bennett's death, and he should therefore have shrunk from resisting as he did. He knew perfectly well when he was locked in deadly conflict with his victim that he was attempting to injure a man who in the name of the law sought to take him into custody, and though every consideration must be given to that natural human impulse to resistance which comes over an individual so circumstanced, it must also be remembered that to molest a Policeman in the execution of his duty is to incur the heaviest penalties.

As the prosecution urged with full force, anybody that kills a Policeman while resisting arrest is according to statute and precedent, guilty of wilful murder, and there can be no doubt that there was a time, even if it has now gone by, when the law was necessary in order to afford adequate protection to officials who have at the best a difficult and dangerous duty to perform. Thus, it is plain that the whole case turned upon the question whether Bennett was in the execution of his duty when he met his death, hence the importance of all evidence as to Bennett's belief on entering the house respecting a felony having been committed.

The Judge held that Bennett was not justified in attempting to arrest Kitts and intimated that Policeman generally are too ready to arrest people whom they consider have broken the law. The charge of murder thus broke down, and the jury acquitted the prisoner of the lesser crime of manslaughter. We are not disposed to call his Lordship's decision in question for it concerns the interpretation of the spirit of the statutes, and in a purely legal matter his Lordship of course speaks with authority. But the importance of the case is great, and if Mr Justice Quain's observation respecting the conduct of the guardians of the peace was warranted the attention of the people most concerned cannot be too carefully directed to it.

There is the consolation in Bennett's case that he doubtless believed he was doing his duty, and if he was guilty of an error of judgement it was an error for which he has paid dearly. It cannot be said that the verdict leaves any stain upon his memory.

-----------------0------------------

Printed in Great Britain
by Amazon